SIMON WILLIS

SCOTTISH

SEA KAYAK

TRAIL

First published 2009

Published in Great Britain 2009 by Pesda Press
Unit 22, Galeri
Doc Victoria
Caernarfon
Gwynedd
LL55 1SQ

© Copyright 2009 Simon Willis

ISBN: 978–1–906095–17–8

Printed and bound in Poland. www.polskabook.pl

To Liz,

for opening up a new world.

Warning

Sea kayaking is inherently a potentially dangerous sport. With this considered, users of this guide should take the appropriate precautions before putting to sea.

The information supplied in this book has been thoroughly researched; however the author can take no responsibility if tidal times differ or if the information supplied is not sufficient to negotiate the conditions experienced on the day. Conditions can change quickly and dramatically on the sea and there is no substitute for utilising personal experience and good judgement when kayaking or (arguably even more importantly) whilst planning a sea trip.

The guide is no substitute for personal ability, personal risk assessment and good judgement. Remember that the outdoors cannot be made risk free and that you should plan and act with care at all times for your own safety and that of others. The decision on whether to go out sea kayaking or not, and any consequences arising from that decision, remain yours and yours alone.

Contents

Foreword

Scotland's west coast, together with the Hebrides and the Northern Isles, constitutes one of the best recreational sea-kayaking environments in the world. This explains why people have been paddling there for almost 140 years and the first circumnavigation of the mainland, from the Solway to the Tyne, took place over a century ago. Those early canoeists ventured into the exciting and challenging waters in craft not all that different from the sea kayaks of today, but without the benefits of purpose-designed clothing, buoyancy aids, dry suits and certainly without guidebooks.

A relative newcomer, Simon took up sea kayaking in 2003 as an experienced outdoor man and hill-walker escaping the overcrowded hills. Like others from a similar background, he has found sea kayaking to have many advantages. The ability to practice his new-found skills in magnificent scenery combines well with photography and the enjoyment of a varied wildlife; from seals and whales to sea birds, otters and deer.

Simon brings with him an enthusiasm and a desire to pass on the benefits of his experiences to others. Sea kayaking is currently enjoying a tremendous surge in numbers of participants. This, combined with the pace of modern life and its demand for instant information, if not at the touch of a button at least at the turn of a page, gives Simon the raison d'être for his guide. The Scottish Sea Kayak Trail contains almost all the practical knowledge required for the recommended trips.

While this book provides much valuable information, it should be regarded as just another item of equipment for the paddler and cannot replace good judgement. What is missing, quite deliberately, is the string of pearls along the trail. The identification of each perfect beach or campsite would create a honey pot effect and be bad for the environment.

It is better by far to enjoy the spirit of adventure and find your own pearls. There is no better place in the world to look than along the Scottish Sea Kayak Trail.

Duncan R. Winning OBE. HONORARY PRESIDENT, SCOTTISH CANOE ASSOCIATION.

Preface

It is the long journey that captures my imagination. While I've bagged my share of summits, I've always preferred the long-distance through-route to ticking off another top. Whether I've been carrying a rucksack or pedalling a bike, I have usually chosen the long way around.

In 2002 I walked the length of the United States of America. Together with Liz, who subsequently agreed to marry me, we crossed baking deserts and snow-choked mountain passes following the 2,658 mile Pacific Crest Trail. That journey changed our lives in ways we are still discovering.

After five months continuous backpacking, we wanted to try a new sport, and turned to sea kayaking because it has the sense of journeying we enjoy so much.

Since then kayaking has become a major part of our lives. We have spent most of our free time exploring Scotland's west coast. We changed jobs and moved house to be closer to a prime kayaking area. Spending a summer paddling the length of the coast, so I could write this book, was an obvious progression.

So if you choose to undertake this long kayak journey, expect to move and think at a different pace. When things go wrong, the way you cope will be yet another part of the adventure.

I cannot guarantee the Scottish Sea Kayak Trail will change your life. But it might.

Simon Willis

About Simon and Liz

Thousands of sea kayakers around the world know Simon's voice from his podcast website (SeaKayakRoutes.com) and through his work as a correspondent with the BBC.

Liz was tackling a series of unclimbed peaks in Alaska when she met Simon and kept him on track when they hiked the length of the USA together, following the 2,658 mile wilderness Pacific Crest Trail from Mexico to Canada.

After five months backpacking, they turned to sea kayaking and became passionate advocates for the sport. They moved house and switched jobs so they could live and kayak on Scotland's west coast.

Simon makes adventure films and shoots videos for businesses. He contributes travel articles to newspapers, such as *The Sunday Times* and *The Herald*, as well was writing for specialist magazines. His work has appeared in all the UK's kayaking magazines.

Liz continues to keep Simon on track and endures being photographed more than most kayakers.

Lochailort, just off the trail at Glenuig (page 104).
Photo | Douglas Wilcox.

📷 *Viewed from the Arisaig skerries, a low bank of cloud obscures the hills of Eigg while beyond, the rugged summits of the Rum Cuillin break through (page 105). Photo | Douglas Wilcox.*

About the Trail

The west coast of Scotland offers world-class sea kayaking. The scenery is spell-binding; from cliffs which soar abruptly from the sea, to perfect ribbons of white sand, stretched between scattered skerries along remote coastlines. The full force of the North Atlantic is still shaping the seascape, providing the sea kayaker with exposure and challenge, particularly on remote headlands. There are sheltered waters and swift tidal passages. The trail passes close to numerous villages and a few towns, but the overall atmosphere is of paddling perfection – wild and remote – where you are more likely to enjoy the company of seals and eagles than tourists.

You will also be acutely aware of your place in history. For more than 8,000 years, people have navigated these waters in vessels small and large. Their spirits are everywhere, as are the marks they left on the landscape. From Iron Age settlements to the early Gaelic kingdom of Dalriada; from Viking raiders to the Lords of the Isles; and from the Highland Clearances to the industrialisation of sea fishing, you will find traces of them all. It is no exaggeration to describe this trail as a voyage through history, helping you to understand the story of Scotland.

Your constant companion will be the weather. You may come to regard it as a living, breathing thing, and fickle too. It can be calm and relaxed, yet change its demeanour over the course of a morning. When it loses its temper, it can marshal the forces of wind and waves to halt all progress. Then just when you have hauled your kayak ashore and set up your tent, your capricious companion will enlist the evening sun in a display that leaves you breathless at its beauty. Scotland doesn't seem to have a climate, only weather, and you will come to know each other well.

You and your party will not kayak in isolation. Whether it's the ghosts of the early Gaels, the splash of the seals and dolphins, or the embrace of the elements, you will travel in good company. Treat them all with respect.

THE SECTIONS:

Swift Waters Flowing
Section 1: Gigha to Oban (124km)

'Gigha' probably means God's Island and, as the most southerly of the Hebridean chain, is a logical place to begin the Scottish Sea Kayak Trail. Big skies and vast open seas overpower both the low-lying land and the human senses. The backdrop of Islay and mountainous Jura beckon you afloat. Kayak north, and the coast reclaims some tentative authority, fractured into a series of remote, jagged headlands. Tide races run off some of these, including the infamous 'Dorus Mor', the Great Door. The islands offer some protection from the Atlantic

and also constrict its flow, which runs at up to 14km an hour. You kayak, not when you decide, but when the sea permits.

Marinas hove into view, for this is prime territory for weekend sailors, then villages with historic traces of a long-gone slate quarrying industry. The section ends in one of the busiest tourist towns on the west coast.

For remoteness and the swift tidal waters, this is the second most difficult section, after Northlands, of the Scottish Sea Kayak Trail.

Lords of the Isles
Section 2: Oban to Mallaig (150km)

The first half of this section is largely protected from the Atlantic by the Isle of Mull. Although the cliffs of Morvern are wild and remote, land is always on the horizon. Progress is punctuated by glowering castles, some in ruins, some intact. This is the domain of the Lords of the Isles, powerful clan chieftains who ruled both land and sea. When the trail leaves the picturesque town of Tobermory, its character changes abruptly as it rounds the first great headland of Ardnamurchan Point. To the north, the Small Isles provide a fabulous panorama but little shelter,

and the trail is exposed once again. This makes arrival into the maze of sheltered skerries off Arisaig a welcome relief, albeit a brief sensation, before heading up the coast to the busy fishing and ferry port of Mallaig.

Kayaking from lowlands to highlands, as the mountains rise and the coastline becomes increasingly rugged, makes this a particularly pleasurable section. It is also perhaps the easiest stretch of the Scottish Sea Kayak Trail.

Tip: I have often heard it said with some pride that "Argyll and Bute has a longer coastline than all of France". If you hear this astonishing boast, probably in a bar, you might care to enter into a small wager, then point out it simply isn't true.

According to the Marine and Coastal Development Unit of Argyll and Bute Council, its coastline measures 2,704km while that of France is 3,140km. Those figures include all the islands. When you think about it, that is still very long.

Big Mountains, Big Seas
Section 3: Mallaig to Kyle of Lochalsh (47km)

This is Scotland at its most magnificent: a visual contest between dramatic seascape on one side and soaring mountains on the other. Considered a last great wilderness by some, there are no roads into the rugged peninsula of Knoydart, although a dramatic and tragic history leads from it. The trail crosses the mouths of two large sea-lochs, down which the wind can whip up serious storms. The trail continues, squeezing through the narrowest of gaps between the mainland and the Isle of Skye, where the swift tide can speed you through or halt you in your tracks.

While this section is spectacular and challenging, the short length means it's only a weekend adventure and no harder than Section 2.

Northlands
Section 4: Kyle of Lochalsh to the Summer Isles (156km)

Those seeking remote, challenging kayaking in spectacular mountain scenery will find nothing better in the world than this section of the Scottish Sea Kayak Trail. At first, the dramatic Skye Cuillin provide a spectacular backdrop, followed by the cliffs at the north of the misty isle. Soon they slip behind and only the distant Outer Hebrides, particularly the hills of Harris, are visible on the western horizon. Here the sea kayaker feels very small, camped on vast, bright red beaches or tucked beneath soaring mainland cliffs. The greatest challenges come near the end, in particular, rounding the fearsome headland of Rubha Reidh or the open water crossing to the Summer Isles where, if the weather is not in your favour, you will not pass. The Summer Isles, clustered in the wide mouth of Loch Broom, possess that magical spirit which makes some places so utterly special. You feel the same spiritual quality here as on the Isle of Gigha where the trail begins. There are no buses to the Summer Isles, so the kayaker must head down the loch to Ullapool to plan the return home.

Before embarking upon this section, it must be fully understood that weather conditions may not permit its completion in full. For exposure, remoteness, length and sheer unpredictability, this is the most difficult section of the Scottish Sea Kayak Trail.

 ## Scotland's Story

Each passage is accompanied by 'additional information'. Sometimes it's practical advice but frequently it involves a story or anecdote from history. Throughout the book historical nuggets are sprinkled to distract your mind while your arms and legs do the hard work, hopefully adding an extra dimension to your enjoyment of these superb kayaking waters.

Arriving at Arisaig (page 105). Photo | Douglas Wilcox.

Planning your Trip

Whether you attempt to kayak the whole trail in one expedition or tackle it in sections will largely depend upon the amount of time you can devote to your journey. Paddling speed, length of day, number of rest days and number of days storm-bound are simply too many variables to compute. Add in the unpredictable events which will inevitably crop up and even you will find it difficult to predict how long you will take on any particular section, let alone the whole route.

Flexibility is essential. You can decide how long you have or how far you will go, but not both. If you are determined to complete an entire section, or the whole route for that matter, you must allow a flexible amount of time, far more than might initially seem necessary. If your time is fixed then you must be flexible in how far you paddle, understanding before you begin that you might not be able to complete your chosen route.

Alternative options are provided for shuttling around areas that, in bad weather, are likely to become impassable. To choose a bad weather alternative is not an admission of failure, but common sense. Any multi-day journey by sea kayak on this superb cost will be rewarding. Keep that at the forefront of your thoughts while deciding how to tackle this trail.

When to go

The sea kayak 'season' on Scotland's west coast runs from April to October. Although the region enjoys some superb winter days, outside of these dates it is rare to experience more than two days in a row of settled weather. As our climate changes it becomes harder to predict which part of the 'season' will be best for tackling the Scottish Sea Kayak Trail.

May usually brings a mix of superb and dreadful kayaking weather. For most of the year, the prevailing wind is between south and west, but anticyclones tend to become more established in May and June, bringing those months a greater share of north and easterly winds, which may hinder progress. July and August are usually warmer, which can make kayaking more uncomfortable, and these months also bring more rain. The years when a large, stable high pressure sat over the west coast for a week or two appear to be gone. Nevertheless, July and August may seem to be the best months for attempting the Scottish Sea Kayak Trail, were it not for another important factor.

The Highland midge becomes active at the end of May, spends June getting up to strength and by July and August can drive the hardiest of campers into a screaming mass of arm-whirling, beast-swatting rage. There are thirty types of midge but the little devil responsible for most tourist misery is the female *Culicoides Impunctatus*, as the male doesn't bite. They do not behave like solitary mosquitoes. These small, biting insects hunt in swarms, clogging your nose, eyes and ears, reminding you of your place in the food chain.

If one or two squeeze into your tent you may not see or hear them, and only become aware of their presence when you wake covered in small, red, itchy boils. Some people have an even more violent allergic reaction. Midges love still, damp, overcast or shady conditions and are most active around sunrise and sunset, just the time you will be landing, setting up the tent and catching the last rays of the day. They can't cope with wind or heavy rain, so perversely you might find yourself hoping for bad weather. You will become expert at locating campsites on promontories or raised ground to catch any breeze and your tent must have midge-proof netting on the doors.

Repellents with DEET are effective but some people believe the chemicals to be harmful and prefer to use natural products. DEET is a solvent which can damage equipment, such as dry suit seals and groundsheets.

Tip: Expect midges, so keep your head-nets handy at sea and on land. If the weather is calm, camp on exposed ground to catch any breeze. Once the tent is up, before opening the door, light an anti-mosquito smoke coil and place it in the porch for a couple of minutes. Keep the anti-midge netting shut while inside or keep a coil burning in the porch. Before retiring to bed, prepare coils for lighting in the morning in case the wind drops overnight. You should carry a complete covering of midge-proof shore clothing.

So the choice is this: May and June avoids the midges but strong head-winds are more likely; July and August are warm but are more likely to be wet, and midges can make camping unpleasant. There is simply no way of knowing in advance when a period of perfect paddling weather will arrive. This uncertainty has the welcome effect of spreading the impact of sea kayakers across the summer months.

OBAN AREA	JAN	FEB	MAR	APR	MAY	JUN	JUL	AUG	SEP	OCT	NOV	DEC
Max Temp (°C)	7	7	9	11	15	16	18	18	15	13	9	8
Hours of sun	34	60	86	146	190	175	143	142	98	76	46	31
Rainfall (mm)	192	140	153	80	67	83	102	119	163	187	182	192
Wind (mph)	12	12	12	10	9	9	8	8	9	10	11	12

Seasonal weather conditions around Oban.

Logistics

Getting back to where you started from is one of the biggest difficulties of kayaking from A to B. Since public transport in some places is limited to one bus every other day, and hitch-hiking can frequently be the only option, time must be factored into the journey. Fortunately, trains and buses are more frequent in the towns at the start and end of each section, but even so, the shuttle takes careful planning.

If you are tackling two consecutive sections, then you will probably wait until you have finished both before returning to collect your car. However, if you are tackling three or all sections, it's probably worth using a rest day to move the vehicle closer to where you are paddling, in case of emergencies.

Each chapter ends with a recommended descrip-tion of how to manage the shuttle back to the start of that section, leaving plenty of scope for creative use of trains, buses and ferries. The grid overleaf puts all the information in one place. Find the place you wish to depart from in the rows and then find the place you wish to return to in the columns. Where the row and column intersect are instructions of how to manage that shuttle.

If you experience extended periods of bad weather, you might need your vehicle to skip ahead and move your kayaks further along the trail. For two major obstacles in Section 2 and Section 4, advice is given.

Keep the number for Traveline Scotland handy (0870 200 2233) as their operators can find the best route between two places by public transport.

FERRIES	Caledonian MacBrayne	0870 565 000	www.calmac.co.uk
	Arisaig Marine (Small Isles Tours)	01687 450224	www.arisaig.co.uk
	Bruce Watt (Knoydart ferry)	01687 462320	www.knoydart-ferry.co.uk
TRAIN	First Scotrail	0845 755 0033	www.firstscotrail.com
	National Rail	08457 48 49 50	www.nationalrail.co.uk
COACH/BUS	Scottish CityLink	0870 550 5050	www.citylink.co.uk
	West Coast Motors	0870 850 6687	www.westcoastmotors.co.uk
	Shiel Buses	01967 431272	www.shielbuses.co.uk
	Post Buses	08457 740740	www.royalmail.com/postbus
	Westerbus (Gairloch)	01445 712255	www.celticfringe.org.uk/postbus.htm
	ScotBus (Gairloch)	01463 224410	www.scotbus.co.uk
	Ewen's Coaches	01854 612966	www.ewensofullapool.co.uk
	Highland Country Buses	01463 710555	www.rapsons.co.uk
PLANNING	Highland Council	01463 702 660	public.transport@highland.gov.uk
	Argyll & Bute Council	01546 604360	public.transport@argyll-bute.gov.uk
	Traveline Scotland	0871 200 2233	www.travelinescotland.com
	Scottish Sea Kayak Tail		scottishseakayaktrail.com

Transportation, useful numbers and links.

Map locations: ULLAPOOL, INVERNESS, KYLE OF LOCHALSH, MALLAIG, FORT WILLIAM, TYNDRUM, OBAN, LOCHGILPHEAD, TAYINLOAN

	GIGHA FERRY	OBAN	MALLAIG	KYLE OF LOCHALSH
OBAN	Bus service 423 Oban to Lochgilphead. Coach 926 Lochgilphead to Tayinloan. Walk 10m to Gigha Ferry. Drive 2hr back to Oban.			
MALLAIG	Train or bus (service 1 or 500) Mallaig to Fort William. Then by coach 918, Fort William to Oban (915 via Tyndrum on Sat morning). Then bus service 423, Oban to Lochgilphead. Then coach 926, Lochgilphead to Tayinloan. Walk 10min to Gigha Ferry then drive 4hr 45 min back to Mallaig.	Train or bus (service 1 or 500) Mallaig to Fort William. Coach 918 Fort William to Oban (915 via Tyndrum Sat morning). Walk 10min to car. Drive 2hr 45min back to Mallaig.		
KYLE OF LOCHALSH	Coach 915 Kyle to Fort William. Coach 918 Fort William to Oban (915 via Tyndrum Sat morning). Bus service 423 Oban to Lochgilphead. Coach 926 Lochgilphead to Tayinloan. Walk 10m to Gigha Ferry. Drive 5hr 45min back to Kyle.	Coach 915 Kyle to Fort William. Coach 918 Fort William to Oban (915 via Tyndrum Sat morning). Walk 10min to car. Drive 3hr 45min back to Kyle.	Coach 915 Kyle to Fort William. Train or bus (service 1 or 500) Fort William to Mallaig. Drive 3hr 30min back to Kyle.	
ULLAPOOL	A two day journey. By coach 961, Ullapool to Inverness. Coach 919, Inverness to Fort William then coach 918, Fort William to Oban (915 via Tyndrum on Sat morning). Day two – bus service 423, Oban to Lochgilphead. Then coach 926, Lochgilphead to Tayinloan. Walk 10m to Gigha Ferry then drive 7hr 30min back to Ullapool.	Coach 961 Ullapool to Inverness. Coach 919 Inverness to Fort William. Coach 918 Fort William to Oban (915 via Tyndrum Sat morning). Walk 10min to car. Drive 5hr 30min back to Ullapool	Coach 961 Ullapool to Inverness. Coach 919 Inverness to Fort William. Train or bus to Mallaig. Drive 4hr 30min back to Ullapool.	Coach 961 Ullapool to Inverness. Coach 919 Inverness to Kyle. Drive 4hr back to Ullapool.

You can check these details with Traveline (📞 0871 200 2233). More detailed shuttle information is given at the end of each section.

Tidal streams

On a long kayak journey, your body will become attuned to working in six hour blocks, paddling north when the flood tide is running and resting on the strongest part of the ebb. There are kayaking destinations in the world where negligible tidal streams negate the need for detailed planning. This is emphatically not the case in Scotland.

Before embarking upon any section of the Scottish Sea Kayak Trail, it is essential to understand how to use tide tables and the tidal stream information in this book to calculate current tidal streams. Furthermore, it is vital to understand how these tidal streams will combine with wind and landform to affect sea state. If you are unsure, two books from Pesda Press are recommended:
Sea Kayak Navigation by Franco Ferrero.
Sea Kayak – A Manual for Intermediate & Advanced Sea Kayakers by Gordon Brown.
The tidal streams in this book are described relative to high water at Oban and Ullapool. You will need

tide tables for Oban in section one; tide tables for Ullapool in section three and four; and in section two, you will need both sets of tide tables. Times of High Water can be downloaded from the EasyTide website (easytide.ukho.gov.uk) which gives free predictions up to seven days in advance. Oban and Ullapool tide tables can be found in *Reeds Small Craft Almanac* published by Adlard Coles Nautical, along with a host of valuable information for the whole of the UK. The cheapest sources of information are the small tide table booklets sold in chandlers and marine suppliers.

In complex tidal sections, such as in the Dorus Mor, or for making detours from the trail, it is recommended that you consult additional sources of information such as those suggested later in this chapter. These will allow you to predict, with much greater certainty, how active a tidal stream will be at a specific time. If you use an iPhone the applications *Boatie* and *World Tides* are also useful.

 ## Why's the tide going that way?

Using the best tidal stream information and accurate tide tables, we nevertheless found, in some places, the tide gave us a push when we expected to be battling against it. This is because tidal streams in the middle of some channels can be different to the streams at the sides of the same channel. Because the UK Hydrographic Office information comes from specialist vessels moored in the main part of a channel, and is aimed at larger vessels than kayaks, their experience may be different to ours nearer the coast.

It is advised that you pass most of the difficult tidal sections at slack water as the flow begins to move north, the direction in which you are travelling. The advantage of this approach is that you cross the difficult section when the sea is least active and then enjoy the advantage of having the tide with

you to travel up the coast. However, there are exceptions to this approach.

If the wind is against you, and the difficult section takes longer to negotiate than expected, then travelling with the tide could result in you kayaking into increasingly rougher seas as the tidal stream speeds up. So, if wind is against the tide, consider passing the tricky tidal section at the other slack water. That is to say, as the flow begins to move south, in the opposite direction to which you are travelling, but with the wind. Once through the tricky tidal passage you may have to land and rest for six hours until the flow against you stops and turns, or the wind changes.

 # A voyage through history

Eight thousand years ago, the first humans in Scotland knew well the waters of the Scottish Sea Kayak Trail. In small crafts, they rounded the same headlands and negotiated the channels that you will tackle today.

The west coast shaped Scotland's history. It was a place of comings and goings, from the arrivals of the Gaels and the Norsemen, to the forced departures of entire communities during the Highland Clearances. Understanding a little of this history will go a long way towards appreciating the shape of the land and the character of the people.

Weather and forecasts

Rain makes you and your equipment uncomfortably wet but only a torrential downpour should prevent progress. However, wind is all-powerful. A tail-wind will speed you on your way, while a head-wind can stop you in your tracks. A cross-wind can make it difficult to kayak in a straight line – or even upright! When wind opposes swell or tide, the waves become steep and alter alarmingly the character of the sea. Below cliffs, around headlands, and in sea lochs, changes in wind direction and strength can be sudden and significant, their ferocity amplified by the topography. So while there are key places where tidal streams will dictate the timing of your journey, the wind is probably the most important environmental factor.

Seek regular weather forecasts, know how to interpret them and appreciate that they are only estimations of what might happen. You must keep a constant eye on the weather. The most useful forecasts are the inshore waters bulletins issued by the Met Office on behalf of HM Coastguard.

The UK is divided into nine inshore waters areas that extend twelve miles out to sea. The Scottish Sea Kayak Trail passes through two of these areas: Mull of Kintyre to Ardnamurchan Point; and Ardnamurchan Point to Cape Wrath. HM Coastguard broadcasts the current inshore waters forecast on marine VHF every three hours, and this essential listening punctuates the kayaking day. Broadcasts by Stornoway coastguard can sub-divide its area to give separate forecasts for the Western Isles and the mainland. An initial broadcast on Channel 16 advises the channel number on which the full broadcast will take place. If you miss a forecast and can't wait until the next broadcast, call HM Coastguard by phone or VHF radio and the operator will read it to you. There are many places where VHF and cell phone coverage is poor.

Each broadcast begins with the time of issue. Make a note of it, because this is the time to which the future timings in the broadcast relate using the following terms; 'imminent' means within six hours of time of issue; 'soon' means between six and twelve hours; and 'later' means after more than twelve hours. Further details can be found on the Met Office website (www.metoffice.gov.uk).

Hopefully you'll avoid seas like this. Photo | Patrick Winterton.

HM Coastguard	Broadcast Times							
Clyde ☎ 01475 729 988 (South of Ardnamurchan Point)	0210	0510	0810	1110	1410	1710	2010	2310
Stornoway ☎ 01851 702013 (North of Ardnamurchan Point)	0110	0410	0710	1010	1310	1610	1910	2210

Copy and laminate this grid. Keep it with your marine VHF radio.

Alternative sources

Telephone: You can get a recorded five-day inshore waters forecast from Marinecall on 09068 500 followed by 463 for Mull of Kintyre to Ardnamurchan Point, or 464 for Ardnamurchan Point to Cape Wrath. Calls can be expensive, so check current prices before departure at www.marinecall.co.uk.

WAP (mobile phone): www.xcw1.com gives current wind speed at five locations close to the trail; Campbeltown, Islay, Tiree, Skye, Lusa, and Aultbea, but this isn't much use as a forecast.

Smartphone: The iPhone *Boatie* application gives inshore forecasts and synoptic charts. Other weather applications are becoming available all the time.

Radio: A small radio which receives LW, MW and FM is useful; a twenty-four hour inshore waters forecast is broadcast on BBC Radio Four (198 LW 92 – 96 and 103.5 – 104.9 FM), and on Radio Scotland (810 MW and 92 – 95 FM).

In town: At your hotel or guest house, watch the BBC weather forecast on television. Or go to Ceefax page 409 for the 24 hour inshore waters forecast, although this version only seems to be updated once a day at around 6 am. If you can get online, look at the Inshore Waters section of the Met Office website.

Force[1] (Beaufort)	mph[2]	Ocean wave height (m)	Sea conditions	Kayaking conditions
0	<1	0	Mirror-like.	Easy.
1	1-3	0	Almost mirror-like.	Easy.
2	4–7	0.1	Small wavelets. Crests of glassy appearance, not breaking.	Easy.
3	8–12	0.4	Large wavelets. Crests begin to break. A few white horses.	Relatively easy. Noticeable work into headwind. Novices start to struggle in cross-wind.
4	13–18	1	Small waves. Frequent white horses.	Sustained effort into head-wind. Following wind becomes following sea.
5	19–24	2	Moderate gale. Moderate longer waves. Some foam and spray.	Hard effort. Begin to use low paddling style. Cross-winds become difficult.
6	25–31	3	Large waves with foam crests and some spray.	Very hard effort. Paddle flutter requires control. Limit of practical paddling any distance into head-wind. Following sea requires concentration.
7	32–38	4	Sea heaps up and foam begins to streak.	Strenuous. Following seas exhilarating for experienced kayaker, but risk of capsize for others. Paddling cross-wind very difficult.
8	39–46	5.5	Moderately high waves with breaking crests forming spindrift. Streaks of foam.	Very strenuous. Lots of concentration required downwind. Into the wind for only short distances.
9	47–54	7	High waves with dense foam. Waves crests start to roll over. Considerable spray.	Survival paddling. Seek shelter immediately.
10	55–63	9	Storm. Very high waves. The sea surface is white and there is considerable tumbling. Visibility reduced.	Survival paddling. Seek shelter immediately.

Forecast windspeeds and the conditions you can expect. Adapted from *Sea Kayak* by Gordon Brown.
[1] used by HM Coastguard.
[2] used by the BBC in their broadcasts.

Maps, charts and guidebooks

While the maps in this book will help your planning, when it comes to navigating on the water, Ordnance Survey 1:50,000 Landranger maps are recommended. OS maps are overlaid with a grid of 1km squares, so distances in this book are given in kilometres. The maps required are listed at the start of each section. Mark these with the tidal information found in this book and you will have a sound, although not infallible, basis for navigating the Scottish Sea Kayak Trail.

If you wish to explore a particular area further, consider investing in one of the 1:25,000 Explorer series. For navigating entire sections these probably have too much detail and would be too expensive.

You should carry, and know how to use, a simple hand-held, orienteering compass. A deck-mounted compass is helpful but not necessary. A GPS in a waterproof bag should be considered almost essential on a multi-day trip, if only to display speed and distance. Take one which uses replaceable batteries which can be bought on route, or experiment with rechargeable batteries and solar chargers.

Using the Garmin GPSmap 76Csx with waterproof case.

 ## Our GPS

I use a Garmin GPSmap 76Csx which is a quite bulky and expensive unit. It can be pre-loaded with digital charts and topos but if you have the Ordnance Survey maps, it's unlikely you will need the electronic versions. This particular GPS unit is useful when crossing open water where there is a risk of lateral drift due to wind or tide, as it will show when you are off-course. The barometer is handy for predicting weather trends and the big numbers are easy to read through a waterproof case.

Although the unit is waterproof to IXP7 standard, which means it should survive 30 minutes immersed, this is not a particularly demanding standard. Whatever GPS unit you use, I recommend keeping it in a waterproof bag.

Admiralty Charts provide more detail about the tidal streams you will encounter along the route. When describing tidal streams in this book, only the maximum rate of flow at spring tide has been given. If you wish to calculate with greater precision the rate of flow you might encounter on a specific day at a specific time, then a chart will offer far more information. Of course, performing such calculations requires knowledge and experience, as does interpreting a chart. What is more, charts are more than double the price of OS maps.

In the coastal waters of the Scottish Sea Kayak Trail, where it is comparatively easy to locate yourself relative to distinctive land shapes, contour lines are particularly helpful. For this reason, and for the reason of cost, navigating the trail using Ordnance Survey 1:50,000 Landranger maps is recommended.

Admiralty Sailing Directions – West Coast of Scotland Pilot NP66 (£40) www.ukho.gov.uk

Although aimed at larger vessels, the tidal stream information is useful to sea kayakers, but has no greater detail than this book.

Clyde Cruising Club Sailing Directions www.clyde. org; *Kintyre to Ardnamurchan* (for Sections 1 and 2); *Ardnamurchan to Cape Wrath* (for Sections 2, 3 & 4). Aimed at leisure sailors, these guides use the same colour scheme as Admiralty charts and incorporate some tidal steam atlas information for sections where it is particularly useful.

Imray – The Yachtsman's Pilot (£25) www.imray. com; *Clyde to Colonsay* (for Section 1)

Isle of Mull and adjacent coasts (for Sections 1 and 2); *Skye and Northwest Scotland* (for Section 2, 3 & 4). Also aimed at leisure sailors, Imray guides have their own colour schemes. Aerial photographs are useful and the author appears to have sourced additional tidal stream information.

For day-trips and detours from the Scottish Sea Kayak Trail, Pesda Press publishes a number of sea kayak guidebooks:

Scottish Sea Kayaking, Fifty Great Sea Kayak Voyages by Doug Cooper & George Reid (ISBN 09547061-2-9) is particularly good.

Argyll & the South West, Ardnamurchan to the Solway Firth by Sea Kayak by Douglas Wilcox (ISBN 978-1-906095-19-2)

The Outer Hebrides, A Sea Kayaker's Guide by Robert Emmot, Tim Pickering & Mike Sullivan (ISBN 978-1-906095-09-3)

Northwest Highlands, A Sea Kayaker's Guide by Cailean Macleod (ISBN 978-1-906095-14-7)

As essential reading for preparation and technique I'd recommend:

Sea Kayak Navigation by Franco Ferrero

Sea Kayak Handling by Doug Cooper

Sea Kayak by Gordon Brown.

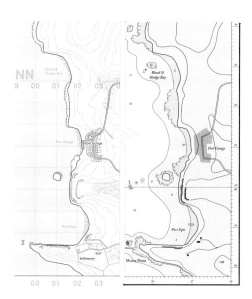

Comparison of Ordnance Survey Landranger map and Admiralty Leisure Series chart styles (both 1:50,000 scale). OS maps also have a latitude scale along the outer edge of the sheet. From *Sea Kayak Navigation*, by Franco Ferrero.

Gaelic for sea kayakers

Gaelic used to be the first language of Scotland's west coast. After years of decline, there are now only around 60,000 native Gaelic speakers. However, numbers are increasing and there's a growing confidence and interest in the language. Much of it is centred on Sabhal Mor Ostaig, the Gaelic College situated on the Sleat peninsula of Skye.

While you might hear Gaelic spoken you're not obliged to learn the language as almost all Gaelic speakers also speak English. But since many place-names are Gaelic, or derived from Gaelic, knowledge of a few words can improve your navigation and even help predict sea conditions.

For example, Garbh Reisa is just another island name but knowing Garbh means 'rough', gives you a clue that the passage between the island and the mainland might be difficult – the tide runs at 8kn.

The words below are for navigational rather than conversational purposes.

Colours

Dubh, dhubh, dubha — black
Geal, gheal — white
Ban, bhan — fair
Buidhe, buie — yellow
Dearg, deirge, ruadh — red
Garbh, garbha, gharbh — rough
Glas, ghlas — grey
Gorm, ghorm — blue
Liath, leithe — grey
Uaine — green

Landform

Abhainn, alit — river, stream
Ard, aird — promontory
Bagh — bay
Camus, camas — bay
Caol, caolas, kyle — narrows
Creag, creige — cliff
Fasgadh — shelter
Rubha, rhu — point of land
Sgeir — rock above water
Uamh — cave

Size & shape

Mor, mhor, mhoir — large
Beag, bheag — small
Fada — long
Ord — round

N Map legend

section start/launch	△	campsite	🏕
landing	◎	tourist information	ⓘ
ferry	🚢	public toilets	🚻
car ferry	🚢	large shop/supermarket	🛒
SYHA hostel	▲	medium shop	🏪
parking	Ⓟ	small shop	🏪

An historic monument on the Summer Isles (page 142).

Fires below tide line only. Photo | Patrick Winterton.

Another use for Werner paddles. (Camp craft, page 45).

The Skye ferry (page 122). Photo | Cailean Macleod.

A subtle 'no camping' sign?

Crystal clear waters and white shell sand beaches are characteristic of the Arisaig skerries(page 105). Photo | Douglas Wilcox.

Safety & Equipment

Boat and paddle

Provided it is sea-worthy, comfortable over long distances, and can hold all your equipment, choice of kayak is entirely personal. Being sea-worthy means that it should have sealed bulkheads and deck-lines, be of a design that can cope with varied sea conditions and the cockpit should seal with a spray-deck. A long river boat is not suitable.

A more important consideration for those flying from overseas is where they can rent a sea kayak. The answer changes year from year and you will find the latest information at the companion web-site www.scottishseakayaktrail.com.

The paddle should be of a style, length and shape you are used to, or you risk aches and blisters. Unless you are comfortable with both your kayak and paddle it could be like striding out on a multi-day hike in brand new boots. Each pair of kayakers should carry at least one spare split-paddle.

 ## Boats & blades

We were delighted with our P&H Cetus kayaks. Less lively than our usual boats, they nevertheless edged and turned well. Their stability was welcome when taking photographs and for cranking out the miles in mixed conditions. Their large capacity meant that we could carry food for ten days, plenty of water and even video equipment.

In preparation for our journey, we each invested in two pairs of Werner foam core paddles. While these were exceptionally light, they didn't fly out of our grasp in high winds. We each had a large (Ikelos) and a medium size blade (Cyprus), expecting we would switch to the smaller blades when tired at the end of the day. As it turned out, we used the Cyprus for almost the entire journey.

Clothing on the water

'Dress for the swim', is a phrase often used by kayakers on Scotland's west coast. For day trips, it's good advice, but harder to follow on a long trail. Summer air temperatures can be high while the water temperature remains low, so dressing for the swim would mean kayaking in far too many clothes. You could dissolve in a puddle of sweat. There's no easy compromise, but this was our approach.

 ## Tops & bottoms

We each carried a good quality, breathable Palm dry suit, which we wore when the weather was wet and cold, or the sea was particularly rough. We adjusted our temperature with several base layers of different thickness. Most of the time we kayaked in Yak salopettes and a thin waterproof Palm cag, a combination that proved suitable for use both on the water and around camp. On the hottest days, which were usually the calmest, we left our dry suits rolled up in a dry bag and wore the salopettes with only a base layer, pulling on the thin cags during showers. A pair of Lomo neoprene boots with a strong sole was the ideal footwear for both combinations, although we occasionally wore Wellington boots with our salopettes, on and off the water. A personal floatation device should be worn at all times. While a wide brimmed sun hat would be essential one day, the next day we might have to switch to a warm, waterproof hat, so we took both. Pogies and gloves should not be necessary in summer unless you are particularly prone to cold hands, so we left them behind.

This combination continues to work well for us, but kayak clothing is as personal a matter as the sea kayak itself.

Clothing off the water

Wicking base layers for top and bottom are ideal both on and off the water, always keeping at least one set of clothes, including socks, completely dry. In addition, carrying a fleece shirt, hat and gloves, and perhaps a down sweater for chilly nights are also recommended, as well as shorts and sandals for hot days.

You will need some light waterproofs around camp. Light cags and salopettes are ideal for light showers and save your drysuit, or seek shelter in your tent in the event of heavy rain. SealSkinz waterproof socks turn sandals into waterproof shoes and can also be worn inside cold neoprene boots.

Wearing layers of clothing will help you stay comfortable.

You also have to consider what you will wear around the supermarket, guesthouse or on public transport during the vehicle shuttle. If you catch the bus wearing shorts over a pair of long johns, and long waterproof socks tucked into neoprene boots, expect a few stares from the other passengers and passers-by.

Security

If you are kayaking more than one section of the Scottish Sea Kayak Trail, you may have to leave your kayaks unattended in a village or town whilst you re-supply, organise lodgings and explore. It's wise to carry a short length of chain and a padlock, or take a bike lock, having first established how you will lock the boats together. P&H Sea Kayaks come with small metal plates fitted behind the cockpit for this purpose.

Secure locking point. The seat post may be another option.

Safety

What's most likely to keep you safe, or be useful in an emergency, are the people you are kayaking with. They should be involved in every aspect of the trail, from planning to paddling. Solo-kayaking the Scottish Sea Kayak Trail is not recommended.

It obviously helps if the kayakers are about the same standard and speed, and aspire to cover the same distances each day. Calculate tidal streams together, or at least check each other's figures, so that you all understand the passage ahead. Two brains are better than one, so discuss forecasts and the effect the wind, tide and land will have on the sea. Any one of you should be able to say "no" to kayaking on any day or through any passage without the others taking offence.

Long before departure, you should have practised together a range of different rescue, self-rescue and towing techniques. If you can't re-enter and roll, consider carrying an inflatable paddle float,

but practise using it in a variety of sea conditions. If you're unsure which techniques you will need, study and practice those set out in *Sea Kayak – A Manual for Intermediate & Advanced Sea Kayakers* by Gordon Brown. It also has advice on putting together a first-aid kit and boat repair kit.

From a jellyfish sting to a boat holed on a rock to a hatch cover blowing off due to heat expansion, or you all ending up in the water, work through 'what if' scenarios with your partners, until you are satisfied that you all have the knowledge and equipment to deal with them.

Practice paddling with your kayak partially filled with water and check if you can pump out your cockpit in a rough sea. If you have thought through how you might handle different situations in advance, you will not only be more confident in rough water, you will stand a much better chance of solving each problem, should it actually occur.

Emergency exit

If you have to divert from or leave the trail for un-planned reasons, use the OS map to work your way to a community. Local people understand what it's like to live with an infrequent or non-existent public transport service so, in an emergency, don't be afraid to ask for help.

Carry some 20p coins and a phone card to use the increasingly rare public telephones and a few pound coins to reimburse people whose own phone you borrow. Have with you the telephone numbers of bus, coach and other transport companies, or even print out their timetables from the web before leaving. The most useful number is Traveline Scot-land (0871 200 2233), as it can provide timetable information for the whole country.

Raising the alarm

In case it all goes horribly wrong you must carry equipment with which to summon help. There are a greater variety of flares available than listed here, including white collision flares, mini-flares, and separate smoke and pin-point flares. Some kayakers argue a Personal Locator Beacon (PLB), such as a McMurdo Fastfind Plus, is not necessary in a relatively well-populated area like the west coast of Scotland but I have one stowed in the rear pocket of my PFD. The SPOT locator system is more advanced, in that it allows people to track your progress online and you can send different types of signal, either 'all is well', 'we're having problems' or 'distress', but it requires an annual subscription.

Alert System	How it works
Marine VHF	Mayday call on Channel 16. There are numerous places where you can hear the Coastguard's powerful radio, but they cannot hear your far less powerful broadcast.
Mobile phone (cell phone)	Put both coastguard offices on speed-dial. There are many places where there is no cell-phone coverage.
Personal Locator Beacon (PLB) or Emergency Position Indicator Radio Beacon (EPIRB)	Used by increasing numbers of kayakers as they get cheaper. Sends GPS co-ordinates to satellite and action taken within 5 mins.
SPOT satellite messenger	Sends GPS signal through commercial satellite network to an emergency centre which contacts relevant authorities. Can also send 'all-is-well' signal and allow GPS tracking online.
Red Parachute Flare (1 each minimum)	Fires rocket 300m into sky which burns bright red for a minute as it slowly descends by parachute. Requires someone to see it and raise the alarm.
Combined Day & Night Flare (1 each minimum)	Used when your rescuer gets close. Release on downwind side of kayak. Day—dense orange smoke, which stains and tastes awful, billows from one end for about a minute. Night—a red pinpoint flare which gets very hot, so hold well down the case.

Rescue

Rescues at sea are co-ordinated by HM Coastguard. Two Coastguard stations cover the Scottish Sea Kayak Trail: Clyde Coastguard (☎ 01475 729988) covers the south of the trail up to Ardnamurchan Point, after which it's the territory of Stornoway Coastguard (☎ 01851 706796).

In an emergency they can be called by dialling 999 on a telephone and asking the emergency operator for 'coastguard', or by issuing a Mayday or Pan-Pan broadcast on VHF Channel 16. The correct procedure is explained during the course that must be taken by anyone seeking a license to operate a marine VHF radio in the UK, and is outlined in short form here. The radio unit itself should also have a licence, available free from Ofcom.

Those are the rules, but if you raised the alarm without having attended a course or using an unregistered radio it's highly unlikely that you would be prosecuted. The reality is you need a marine VHF radio on this trail for receiving weather forecasts and in case of an emergency.

Type of call	When to use
'Mayday' Distress call	Use when a boat or person is threatened by grave and imminent danger, and requires immediate assistance. Call has absolute priority and all other communication stops. It's possible a nearby vessel, with a more powerful radio, will relay a kayak Mayday call if the Coastguard cannot receive your signal.
'Pan-pan' Urgency call	Use to convey a very urgent message about the safety of a person or boat (or other form of transport) or when medical advice is urgently required. Safety is urgent but not yet a matter of grave and imminent danger.
'Securité' Safety call	Used to convey important navigational, meteorological or other safety information to another vessel or to all stations.

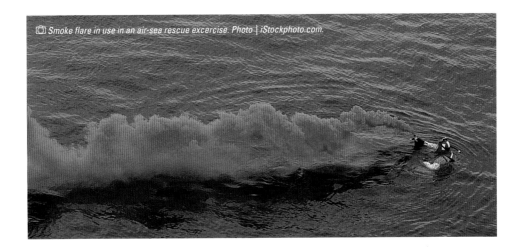
Smoke flare in use in an air-sea rescue excercise. Photo | iStockphoto.com.

How to make a distress call

Switch on the VHF radio. Select Channel 16 and select High Power.

Hold down handset button and say, slowly and clearly:

"Mayday, mayday, mayday."

"This is Kayak ... ..." (repeat boat name three times).

"Mayday Kayak ..." (say boat name once).

Give your position as a grid reference, or latitude and longitude,
or distance and bearing from an obvious point.

"My position is off Arisaig, half a kilometre west of Luinga Mhor, grid reference 600858"

(57°54'·1N 5°57'·3W) or (one third of a nautical mile, 270 degrees west of Luinga Mhor).

Tell them what is wrong.

"We are two people in water, one boat lost and one shoulder injury."

If there is time, repeat your position then tell them what you need.

"We require immediate assistance. Over." (Over means 'please reply'.)

Only if you can't hear clearly, adjust the volume and/or squelch.

If no response, check radio switches and transmit again.

HM Coastguard will want to know your position, which you can give as a grid reference, in latitude and longitude, or your bearing off a known point. Give the nature of the incident, the number of people involved and any additional relevant information. The coastguard will decide which resources to task to the rescue, and can call upon cliff rescue teams, helicopters and the Royal National Lifeboat Institution (RNLI).

Firing a red flare or triggering an electronic locator beacon is the equivalent of broadcasting a Mayday call, except you won't know if anyone has responded until help arrives.

📷 The sun dips into the sea north
of Applecross (page 131).

Campsite near Isle Martin on the final leg to Ullapool (page 144).

Overnight

Finding accommodation

It is difficult to make reservations for hotels, hostels, guest houses and bed and breakfasts along the Scottish Sea Kayak Trail because it's impossible to accurately predict where you will be on any given day. You could speed along on brisk tail winds or be storm-bound for a weekend on an isolated headland. Since the kayaking and tourist seasons coincide, you will be lucky to walk into an inexpensive B&B near the water and convenient for kayaking, but it does happen. Below is a guide to the prices you could expect to pay in 2008.

Wild camping is an essential element of this trail. It's essential because there are many places where there are no other forms of accommodation or habitation. In Sections 1, 2 and 4 there are also formal campsites with showers and other facilities. I highly recommend planning to camp almost every night and only book accommodation for special treats or to organise a shuttle.

When you do need to book accommodation, you might seek advice from the Tourist Information Centres that are run by Visit Scotland. Not many staff will be familiar with the needs of sea kayakers, but if you telephone in peak season with specific requirements, such as needing a place to store a kayak for several days, they might offer a few phone numbers to try. However, don't expect miracles.

Accommodation per person per night	
Hotel (incl. breakfast)	£30 upwards
Guest House (incl. breakfast)	£25 – £55
B&B	£18 – £45
Hostel / Bunkhouse	£14 – £18
Campsite	£8 – £15

Wooden 'wigwams' at Applecross (page 131).

Formal campsites

VISIT SCOTLAND OFFICES		
Lochgilphead (covers Gigha)	📞 01546 602344
Oban	📞 01631 563122
Fort William	📞 01397 701801
Ullapool	📞 01845 612486

No matter how busy they are with touring caravans and large frame tents, most organised campsites welcome backpacker tents. Compared to other forms of accommodation, they're still relatively cheap (£8–£15 for two people), and worth using if only for the showers to rinse salt off clothing, re-supply with fresh water, visit a café and for sorting out equipment.

📷 Port Ban campsite near the start of the trail (page 67).

Wild camping

The delight of pitching your tent on a remote shore is an essential ingredient of this trail. However wild camping must be done responsibly, with every effort made to minimise environmental impact, or the special quality of those remote places will be destroyed. As such, the locations of wild camping and picnic spots are not given in this guide.

Follow the Scottish Canoe Association guidelines; *Wild Camping Advice for Canoeists* and *Human Sanitation Advice*, which can be found online.

Wild camping & Scottish law

The Code confirms access rights extend to wild camping which it defines as follows:

This type of camping is lightweight, done in small numbers and only for two or three nights in any one place. You can camp in this way wherever access rights apply, but help to avoid causing problems for local people and land managers by not camping in enclosed fields of crops or farm animals, and by keeping well away from buildings, roads or historic structures. If you wish to camp close to a house or building, seek the owner's permission.

Leave no trace by taking away all your litter; removing all traces of your tent pitch and of any open fire (follow the guidance for lighting fires); and by not causing any pollution.

Scottish access rights

Scotland has a different legal system to that of England and Wales, and a more open attitude to access. However, the law is still quite new and not all land managers know or adhere to the Code. Because wild camping is an essential part of the Scottish Sea Kayak Trail, you should know your rights and responsibilities.

Part 1 of the Land Reform (Scotland) Act 2003 gives everyone a statutory right of access to most land and inland water, including mountains, moorland, woods and forests, grassland, margins of fields in which crops are growing, paths and tracks, rivers and lochs, the coast, as well as most parks and open spaces. This right can be exercised at any time of the day or night, for recreational purposes, educational purposes, some commercial purposes and for crossing over land or water. People only have these rights if they exercise them responsibly by respecting people's privacy, safety and livelihoods, and Scotland's environment.

The Scottish Outdoor Access Code (available online at www.outdooraccess-scotland.com) provides detailed guidance on your responsibilities and of those managing land and water. While failure to comply with the Code is not an offence, legally it has 'evidential status', which means it can be used to determine whether people are acting responsibly or not.

Camped in Knoydart.

Camp craft

Skill improves with practice. While the idea of camp craft sounds rather old fashioned, it is even more important nowadays with more people seeking out the delights of wild places.

Consider other people and animals: Choose a site suitable to the size of your group, camp as unobtrusively as possible and remember people earn a living from the land. Noise travels from a tent and can disturb wildlife and people.

Minimise disturbance to wildlife: The coast is important to birds and animals, most of which breed from April to June, so avoid camping where you might cause a disturbance. If you become aware you are disturbing nesting birds or animals, move. Scraps of food, even buried, attract scavengers that prey on nesting birds, so carry away all food scraps.

Toilet hygiene: Do your business at least 30 metres from fresh or running water, 50 metres from paths and 200 metres from bothies (huts available to all maintained by the Mountain Bothy Asociation) or camp spots. The best way to dispose of excrement is in the sea by going below the high water mark. Another way is to defecate onto a rock, then throw it into the sea, but this takes practice. Alternatively, dig a hole and bury excrement well away from running water, burning toilet paper if it is safe to do so. Immediately afterwards, use a hand sanitising gel or biodegradable soap, but never directly in a stream.

Minimum impact camping: Minimise your own impact and the repeated impact of others by seeking out discreet places to camp rather than overused spots. Leave no trace, such as drainage ditches, and remove all your rubbish and that of others. Don't stay in one spot more than three nights and, if you're unsure about your practice, make an effort to find out what is right then become evangelical about it. Tell your friends.

Roadside camping: It's not wild camping within the definition of the law but it is included in the Code. If near houses, ask residents before pitching your tent. Park on hard ground and walk to your tent rather than drive on vegetation. Avoid sites that are at risk of being overused and take particular care with toilet hygiene.

Camping equipment

Tent: If you're selecting a tent especially for this trail, I recommend you choose a geodesic design which doesn't rely on pegs to keep it upright and can therefore be pitched on soft sand or a pebble beach. The Terra-Nova Superlite Quasar is roomy enough for two, has a door and porch either end, and is light enough to also use when backpacking. Like most geodesic designs it pitches inner first, which gives more internal space but means the inside can get wet if erected in rain. Being able to separate flysheet from inner allows you to carry the wet outer tent in a separate bag to the dry inner tent and also speeds drying. A large porch or two is useful for cooking and storing kit when storm-bound. The single most essential element is a midge-proof net door to keep out the winged beasts.

Tip: Our procedure when making camp is to erect the tent and then, before opening the inner door, start an anti-midge smoke coil burning in the porch. Only when the smoke drives the midges from here do we open the inner door, keeping the midge net door shut as much as possible.

Stove: Gas stoves designed for backpacking are simplest and most convenient along this trail. Replacement canisters with the screw-type valve can be bought in all of the towns at the ends of sections. Gas has the advantage over alcohol and white gas stoves in that the fuel is less likely to leak into food supplies while stored in the kayak tail. However there are environmental considerations as the canisters cannot yet be recycled, so you may wish to investigate other stoves and fuel types.

Sleeping bag: This is a very personal choice, depending upon how warm you sleep, and whether there's a risk your sleeping bag will get wet. Down-filled bags have the best warmth to weight ratio, compressing to a smaller package than bags filled with synthetic insulation. However, synthetic bags stay warm when wet, when down deteriorates into a cold, soggy, mass (a water-repellent cover can be used to help keep the inevitable condensation away from the down filling). Another advantage of synthetic on a long trip is that it can more easily be laundered to remove salt build-up which can make the bag feel permanently damp. While kayaking, store your sleeping bag compressed in sturdy dry-bags.

Sleeping pad: A self-inflating sleeping pad of the type made by Thermarest should ensure a good night's sleep, even on a pebble beach.

Tip: We use the backpacker length, from under the shoulders to the knees, because any longer is a waste and, when rolled, these fit easily into a dry-bag. We carry inflatable pillows and Thermarest 'chairs'. These are little more than a few straps and scraps of fabric but allow the folded pad to be used as a reasonably comfortable chair.

Essentials: Head torch, cutlery, cup, pan(s), water bags and bottle, anti-midge smoke coils, repellent and head nets.

📷 *Midge-proof head net.*

📷 *Driftwood fire circle and a single malt. Photo | seafreedomkayak.co.uk*

Open fires

The Scottish Outdoor Access Code defines your responsibility as follows:

Wherever possible, use a stove rather than light an open fire. If you do wish to light an open fire, keep it small, under control and supervised – fires that get out of control can cause major damage, for which you might be liable. Never light an open fire during prolonged dry periods or in areas such as forests, woods, farmland, or on peaty ground, near buildings, or in cultural heritage sites where damage can be easily caused. Heed all advice at times of high risk. Remove all traces of an open fire before you leave.

The Scottish Canoe Association advises:

It is acceptable to light a fire on a tidal beach as long as you have your fire below the high water mark and are absolutely certain that there is no risk of setting fire to any nearby trees or vegetation. Lighting a fire in the inter-tidal zone means the next high tide will clear away the evidence of your fire and ensure that it is put out.

It is best to avoid lighting a fire. Dead wood is an important habitat for insects and many small animals, and a fire can easily get out of control on peaty soils and dry grass at any time of year.

Food and water

Although this trail feels wild, the area through which it passes is not a wilderness. You will be able to re-supply, buy occasional meals and find accommodation in some of the small settlements and all of the towns. There's no need to start with a kayak stuffed with expensive freeze-dried food and stove fuel unless you're determined to avoid all human contact. That said, if you have particular dietary requirements, or a fondness for a special type of treat, it's best to carry with you what you will need.

To help your planning, I've divided the shops you will find along the trail into four size categories for this guide; **tiny**, **small**, **medium** and **large**. **Tiny** shops sell just a few basics and, while you might buy a pot noodle or tin of beans to see you though one night, you won't be able to re-supply. You ought to be able to buy all you need for a few days in **small** shops, but choice will be very limited and prices will be noticeably higher. **Medium** shops are effectively small supermarkets, which will have all you need at slightly higher prices, whereas **large** shops are big supermarkets which will stock all you need.

Packing a couple of specialist mountaineering-type long-life freeze dried meals into the tail of your kayak and leaving them for emergencies may prove invaluable.

You can also catch food as you kayak. Mackerel are probably the tastiest fish you'll catch with a simple hand line and several mackerel feather lures. You can also pick mussels from vertical rock faces around low water, discarding any which are open before cooking and closed after cooking. Never steal from creels (lobster pots).

Fresh water is the commodity with which you will most frequently need to restock and it's best to do so whenever you visit a shop, café or campsite. While we drink water straight from a high mountain stream, at sea level the risk of contamination is too great. Cryptosporidium, Campylobacter, Aeromonas, E.coli 0157 and Giardia are all gut pathogens than can be caught from drinking infected water in the UK, although the number of cases are low.

One option is to treat it with iodine (eg. PolarPure) or chlorine dioxide (eg. AquaMira). Bear in mind iodine is a poison that builds up over time in your pituitary gland so, if you don't like ingesting chemicals, consider using a water filter or one of the new electronic purification units. You can avoid the need to treat water by each carrying three 10 litre water bags; one in a day hatch, one behind the backrest and one at your feet. This should be enough to last you around five days, depending upon the temperature. If forced to drink water from a stream, check upstream for dead sheep and bring the water to a rolling boil before drinking.

Some things are indispensable.

Mackerel are common from the end of May to September. Both photos | Patrick Winterton.

Excellent fishing on the Summer Isles. Photo | Douglas Wilcox.

Puffins (scarce along this route) can live as long as thirty years or more.

Wildlife

Day to day, travelling the Scottish Sea Kayak Trail, you will encounter wildlife at every twist and turn. Oyster catchers, herons, gulls, cormorants and shags will be with you most days. Manx shearwaters congregate off Rum, while sea eagles and golden eagles patrol the skies over Mull. It is outside the scope of this book to offer a guide to Scottish sea birds, but you can buy a laminated card which features common sea-birds, or a more detailed reference book such as the Collins Bird Guide.

To identify larger marine mammals, try to get hold of a copy of the booklet *Was it a Whale?* by Jay Butler and Anna Levin. Better still, read *Sea Kingdom of Argyll* by Caroline Lathe and Rosalind Jones, both of which are published by the Hebridean Whale and Dolphin trust and sold in their small shop on Tobermory High Street on the Isle of Mull.

Avoiding disturbance

It is most important not to disturb the animals you encounter. Yet sometimes it is very difficult indeed to know whether the bird or seal you are watching is curious about you, naturally defensive or genuinely anxious. It is generally best to allow creatures to approach you, not the other way around, and never chase them.

To better understand the principles involved, the implications for kayakers are given in *The Scottish Marine Wildlife Watching Code* and the more detailed *Guide to Best Practice for Watching Marine Wildlife*, both of which are published by Scottish Natural Heritage. Also recommended is the leaflet *Sea Kayaking – A guide to good environmental practice* from the Scottish Canoe Association.

What does 'avoiding disturbance' mean? The *Guide to Best Practice for Watching Marine Wildlife* defines it as: 'The result of direct or indirect interaction with people that changes the behaviour of an animal or changes the environment, which in turn affects the well-being or survival of an animal in the short, medium or long term.'

Nests are often well camouflaged and underfoot.

Birds

Almost six million seabirds nest on Scotland's cliffs in summer. Around half of the world's population of great skuas and northern gannets come here, as do a third of the Manx shearwaters. Eighteen species of waders over-winter in Scotland and some, such as the knot and bar-tailed godwit, appear to be in decline. The white-tailed sea eagle, the world's fourth largest eagle, was re-introduced in the 1970s and 1980s and is now breeding successfully with around twenty pairs on the west coast.

However, the bird breeding season usually coincides with the best sea-kayaking weather, so although the disturbance we cause is minimal, we should not be complacent.

Possible disturbance: The breeding sites on cliffs, in burrows or directly on the ground, either hidden in vegetation or well camouflaged, can easily be disturbed. If disturbed when breeding, there's a lower chance of juvenile survival. Predators may be attracted by food litter or if birds are flushed from cover.

Signs of disturbance: Birds at sea will usually swim away from you. If you are uncomfortably close, they'll paddle more rapidly, turning their heads from side to side. If they take off or dive, you were too close. Birds on land will typically take off, circle and land once you have gone past. If a bird attempts to draw you away by faking a broken wing, you are too close to a nest. Birds on cliffs indicate they're about to take flight by head turning, bobbing and wing flapping.

Sensitive times and places: The seabird breeding season is around April to mid-July, although

📷 Shags are smaller than cormorants with a steep forehead. Dense bones help diving but hinder take-off.

burrow-nesting Atlantic puffins, shearwaters and petrels may not leave their burrows until August. The times of greatest sensitivity are late afternoon and early evening; the hottest part of the day; wet and cold weather; moonlit nights; and when chicks are in the nest.

Cliff-nesting guillemots, razorbills and kittiwakes are most vulnerable when the adults are scared away from their chicks, which might fall or be taken by predators. Terns, ringed plovers and oystercatchers all nest on shingle shores where they're well camouflaged and easily trampled. Estuaries play host to waders and waterfowl between October and March where undisturbed feeding and resting can be vital to survival. Try to avoid large rafts of eider, shelduck and other duck chicks which can be found at sea during summer, as they are vulnerable if separated. In late summer, they moult and are particularly weak.

Responsible behaviour: If birds are feeding or resting, try to keep at least 50m away. If they are moving, try not to deflect them from their path. Don't separate young from parents. On shore, be alert to the possibility of eggs or young hidden nearby.

How close you can go without causing significant disturbance depends on the species, local circumstances, and how used to people the birds are. Nesting terns, for example, are highly sensitive and disturbance may make them abandon a nest. Puffins are sometimes more tolerant and may approach and leave burrows in the close presence of humans, although you should avoid walking through colonies for fear of collapsing burrows.

◎ *Sea eagle chick. Photo | www.havnomaden.no*

📷 *A curious common seal pup. Photo | Gareth Brown.*

Seals

There are now more seals in Scotland than anywhere else in Europe. More than a third of the world's grey seal population and more than half of the European population live here, along with around 5% of the world's common (also called harbour) seals and more than a third of the European sub-population. Paddle the Scottish Sea Kayak Trail, and you are guaranteed to see seals.

Grey seal identification: These may appear grey, brown or black with dark mottling. They are distinguished from common seals by their nostrils which form a W shape at the tip of their snout, which has a Roman profile. Large groups are often seen sun-

ning themselves on rocks, but will rapidly slip into the sea when a kayak approaches. As you pass, their large faces pop up from the water and stare after you. Pups are white for their first month.

They breed on wave-exposed rocky coasts, sometimes on sand or shingle beaches at the foot of cliffs, often on relatively remote islands. Large groups of pregnant females return to traditional breeding sites in October and November to give birth, and disperse once the breeding season is over. Pups stay on the beach for three weeks before venturing into the sea.

Common seal identification: Like the grey seal,

these can be grey, brown or black. However, they're smaller, their nostrils form a distinctive V shape and their heads are round with a short snout, making their eyes seem large. Pups have the same colouration as adults.

They prefer more sheltered waters and adults tend to stay in a familiar area. The females usually give birth in shallow water, or sometimes on land, in early summer. Pups go into the sea almost immediately after their birth.

Possible disturbance: Susceptibility to disturbance is site specific. Relatively close approaches may be tolerated in one location, but not at all in the next bay. While mothers forage at sea, pups can be left alone and if disturbed may move to a different location, making it difficult for the mother to find them again. However, seals do get used to visitors and learn to recognise particular boats.

Signs of disturbance: The speed at which they move to the water is the key indicator. When alarmed, seals resting on rocks may stampede in the sea, and this obviously constitutes disturbance to be avoided whenever possible. If they slip into the water one by one, they may be curious to get a better look at you, or to ensure you are not threatening. In most cases this is not a problem, although it may become so if they are repeatedly leaving their haul-out sites. Where adults and pups stay together on land, it may be because it is difficult for the pups to move, yet they might still be disturbed.

Sensitive times and places: Common seals produce their pups from June to July, the prime time for the Scottish Sea Kayak Trail, and may be encountered at sea, on sandbanks or rocks throughout the summer, especially during their annual moult in August. Grey seals produce their pups from October to December at traditional breeding sites and the pups may stay ashore for several weeks. Adults and pups disperse in the spring, once weaning and the moult is complete.

Responsible behaviour: Never land or camp near a haul-out or at a breeding colony. Never separate pups from mothers. There's no safe distance applicable for all sites, but try to avoid stampeding seals into the sea.

[◎] *Common seals. Photo | Chris Denehy.*

[◎] *A grey seal. Photo | Chris Denehy.*

Basking sharks

At up to 11m in length, these leviathans are the largest fish in UK waters. Summer seasonal visitors, they're mainly found near tidal fronts where mixing water generates the abundant plankton, freely drifting tiny plants and animals, on which they feed.

Identification: They are often over 6m long, slate grey (although they can appear black) and feed on plant life by moving slowly along the surface of the water with their gaping mouths wide open. You will most likely notice their thick triangular fin cutting through the sea, while their vertical tail fin moves from side to side. They can usually be distinguished from whales and dolphins by the lack of surfacing and diving and their tail which looks like a second fin.

Possible disturbance: They don't breed until they're around 20 years old, and seem relatively unaware of kayaks and boats, which makes them both vulnerable and potentially dangerous. Historically, they were killed for their oil and it has taken many years for over-exploited populations to recover. Since they weigh up to seven tones, collisions can result in injury to both parties.

Signs of disturbance: The most obvious sign is if the basking shark dives, in which case you were too close. Individuals will usually re-surface and continue feeding. Avoid basking sharks performing multiple dives, and watch out for tail lashes. Sudden tail movements may indicate they are about to breach.

Sensitive times and places: They are usually seen in Scottish waters from May to October, with peak sightings in August. Locations where they congregate are also where they reproduce. Stay away from dense groups of basking sharks, particularly where they are swimming nose to tail, or you may upset a courtship.

Responsible behaviour: The distance at which you disturb them partly depends upon the amount of plankton in the water, because while they're busy feeding, they hardly seem to notice the presence of kayaks. As usual, the key is to let them decide how close they want to be to you, approach at an oblique angle rather than directly, and usually no closer than 100m. Do not cut them off by moving across their path and stay away if they're breaching.

Basking shark dorsal fin.

These quiet giants can be quite excitable at times.
Photo | Colin Speedie, Swiss Shark Foundation.

📷 *Common dolphins. Photo | Hebridean Whale and Dolphin Trust.*

Cetaceans

Over the last one hundred years, no fewer than twenty-one species of whales, dolphins and porpoises have been recorded in Scottish waters. This is one of the best places in Europe for watching what are collectively known as 'cetaceans'. Of these, six species are the most common.

Harbour porpoise identification: If you get one glimpse of a small, triangular fin which subsequently vanishes, the chances are it was a harbour porpoise. Typically they are very shy and will not approach kayaks. At 1.8m long, they're smaller than all the dolphins in these waters. Their fin is almost insignificant, and they surface with a tight, circular movement.

Dolphin identification: According to the experts, you might see any or all of the following: the bottlenose, common and Risso's dolphins.

The bottlenose takes its name from its protruding beak-like head. They're mostly grey with a white underside, a prominent curved dorsal fin and can grow to over 3.5 metres. They love to perform gym-nastic displays, leaping out of the water and riding the bow waves of boats.

Smaller than bottlenose or Risso's, common dolphins are identified by distinctive white and yellow patterns along their sides. They travel in large groups of ten to five hundred individuals and are both gymnastic and noisy.

Compared to the other two types, Risso's dolphins seem to have a blunt forehead and a very small beak. Their curved dorsal fin is quite tall, and while they're grey like the bottlenose, they grow paler with age.

Orca identification: You will not need a guide-book to identify these huge animals which can be 10m long. They have distinctive black and white mark-ings and the males have tall dorsal fins. They can be inquisitive, even playful, and are often seen chasing seals, but leave kayakers alone.

Minke whale identification: You might see their long, dark backs rolling through the water with the small, curved fin two thirds of the way along. You won't see their tails, but if you are close, you might catch a glimpse of broad white bands on their flippers. They have a distinctive dive sequence, of three to five short dives then a long one of up to ten minutes.

Possible disturbance: Noise is usually considered a form of disturbance, but some noise is good if it lets the animals know you are coming and from which direction. Feeding cetaceans is not recommended, nor is swimming with them.

Signs of disturbance: The most obvious sign of disturbance is if they move away but there are also subtle indicators, such as bunching together, tail or head slaps on the water surface, prolonged

diving and aggression at each other or watchers. If disturbed, they can make sudden and erratic movements, although these may also be associated with feeding or playing.

Sensitive times and places: Whenever young are present.

Responsible behaviour: Approach indirectly at an oblique angle and let the animals decide if they want to come closer to you. Minimum approach distances are given as 50m for dolphins and porpoises and 100m for whales, although these are only approximate. For mothers and calves, or for animals clearly actively feeding or in transit it's suggested you stay 200–400m away.

Orcas. Photo | Hebridean Whale and Dolphin Trust.

Bottlenose dolphins. Photo | HW&DT.

Minke whales. Photo | HW&DT.

Otters

In Gaelic they're known as *Dobhran* and *Beaste Dubh* (black beast). There are around 8,000 Eurasian otters in Scotland and they belong to the same family as badgers, weasels, stoats, pine marten and mink. They hunt in both fresh and sea-water, so the waters of the Scottish Sea Kayak Trail are ideal. They swim very flat on the water surface and, when diving for prey, the long tail can be clearly seen as it flips over. Otters call to one another in high pitched squeaks or whistles, and make a loud, angry 'whickering' chatter when threatened. On land they run with a lolloping gait, holding their tail off the ground. Territories can be as small as 1–3km of coastline. They live on land in a 'holt', which can be a hole or hollow under tree roots, in a peat bank, under rocks or even an old rabbit warren. Coastal otters eat mainly fish and crabs, but they will eat birds and small mammals.

Otter identification: Their fur is dark brown on the back, paler on the belly and with a cream patch under the chin. They have a long, stout tail, which is thick at the base and works as a rudder in the water. They're easily confused with mink, but are larger (1.2m) and normally extremely shy. Mink fur is dark all over and when wet it looks black and they can have white spots on their upper and lower lips. At 0.3–0.5m, mink are shorter than otters and far more inquisitive.

Possible disturbance: The otter is listed in the International Union for Conservation of Nature's Red Book as 'vulnerable to extinction'. Average life expectancy is only 3–4 years and they first breed when they reach two years old. A typical litter is of one to three cubs, which become independent at eighteen months, but not all survive to adulthood.

The most obvious sign that they are feeling threatened is if they move away. The first sign is a 'head up' behaviour. If in water, the otter will stop swimming and raise itself higher out of the water while looking around, even directly at you, before disappearing from view. On land, the first reaction to disturbance is also to raise its head, and it might vocalise by 'whickering' its threatening call. You may have disturbed a female with cubs nearby, which she could abandon unless you back off.

Sensitive times and places: There is no fixed breeding season and cubs can be born at any time of the year. It all depends upon the availability of food. Females with cubs are particularly sensitive at any time.

Responsible behaviour: No recommended distances are given for viewing otters, you are advised to let them decide how close they want to be. Their strongest senses are smell and hearing, while their eyesight is more efficient underwater. However, they have a good visual memory of their territories, so camouflage and remaining below the skyline is essential for successful otter watching.

On land, look out for otter paths, which are 12–15cm wide, marked with droppings, and run from the shore into dense vegetation or fresh water pools. Avoid camping nearby, which would compromise the otters' route to the sea.

European otter. Photo | iStockphoto.com

Turtles

Five of the world's seven species of marine turtle have been found in UK and Irish waters but they are rarely seen. The most common and the largest is the leatherback turtle which nests on tropical beaches but forages in tropical and temperate water feeding on jellyfish. It's most often seen during August, but between 2002 and 2004 there were only 28 recorded sightings.

Three other species have been recorded around Scotland; the loggerhead, Kemp's ridley and green turtles.

Leatherback turtle identification: Easy to identify because of its size, black colouration with white spots, and pronounced longitudinal ridges on its back. The largest recorded was stranded on a beach in Wales in 1988, weighing 960kg and measuring 2.9m in length.

Possible disturbance: Worldwide turtle populations are declining. They're at risk from marine litter, especially plastic, which they mistake for jellyfish and which can block their gut. Discarded fishing gear may entangle and kill them. They often float on the surface, leaving them vulnerable to collisions.

Signs of disturbance: If disturbed they will dive rapidly.

Responsible behaviour: In you encounter a turtle, don't chase, follow or harass it in any way. Be aware they have powerful flippers and can bite.

Leatherback turtle. Photo | Colin Speedie, Swiss Shark Foundation.

Recording sightings

Cetacean, basking shark and turtle sightings can be recorded with the Hebridean Whale and Dolphin Trust (0800 0858110, email: sightings@hwdt.org) or Seawatch (01865 717276, www.seawatchfoundation.org.uk).

The Shark Trust is one of the more active organisations working for the conservation of sharks, so if you see a 'basker', please let them know. (0870 128 3045, email: sightings@sharktrust.org). Basking shark sightings are also recorded by the Marine Conservation Society (www.mcsuk.org/marineworld/baskingsharks) and also the European Basking Shark Photo-Id Project (www.baskingsharks.co.uk)

Reporting stranded or injured marine wildlife

Scottish Society for the Prevention of Cruelty to Animals (0131 339 0111, www.scottishspca.org) or British Divers Marine Life Rescue (01825 765546, www.bdmlr.org.uk). In the case of a cetacean, please also call Scottish Agricultural College's Veterinary Investigation Centre, part of the National Whale Stranding Recording Scheme (01463 243030 or out of hours 07979 245893). Animals with tags should also be reported to the Sea Mammal Research Unit (01334 462631 www.smru.st-andrews.ac.uk)

Reporting dead animals

Cetaceans, basking sharks and turtles: Scottish Agricultural College's Veterinary Investigation Centre (01463 243030 or out of hours 07979 245893). Seals (especially with tags): Sea Mammal Research Unit (01334 462631 www.smru.st-andrews.ac.uk). Birds: RSPB (0131 311 6500 www.rspb.org.uk)

📷 *Launch at the beach beside CalMac ferry to Gigha (page 63).*

📷 *Superb sunsets with seals, near Port Ban (page 67).*

📷 *Tide race SW corner of Eilean Mor (page 69).*

📷 *Kilberry Castle – mediaeval carved tombstones (page 67).*

📷 *Gylen Castle (page 78).*

Mull
Kerrera • Oban
1.6
• Clachan Bridge

1.5

1.4 • Crinan
• Carsaig

1.3

• Kilberry
1.2
Gigha 1.1
• Tayinloan

Swift Waters Flowing

Section 1: Gigha – Oban (124km)

The Scottish Sea Kayak Trail starts beneath open skies and on exposed seas, and is not typical of kayaking in these waters. One of the delights of Scotland's west coast is that each passage is different to the last, sometimes subtly so, sometimes dramatically. This is what makes kayaking the trail such a marvellous undertaking.

At the start of Section 1, you will find no soaring mountains or busy waterways, although all of these lie ahead. It's the exposure to the Atlantic Ocean you will notice most as you begin to make your way towards the highlands. Hebridean islands crowd in from the west and the tides speed up, becoming the dominant feature. Tide and wind dictate how and when you kayak, particularly around remote headlands. Almost two thousand years ago, this was the Kingdom of Dalriada, a place where Christianity came to Scotland, and the ancient remains of early chapels, crosses and burial sites are easily found. Soon you are in the playground of weekend sailors, as marinas and villages appear along the coast and the sea becomes even more sheltered leading into Oban, the first large town on the trail and the end of this section.

OS Sheets:

62, 55 & 49

Tide tables:

Oban

Useful Charts:

Sound of Jura,
Crinan to Luing and
Loch Craignish,
Sound of Luing

SWIFT WATERS FLOWING

1.0
1.1
1.2
1.3
1.4
1.5
1.6

Travel to the start

There's no fast way from Glasgow to Gigha. The roads start small and get smaller, with even the most direct route taking around three hours to drive. Head north on the A82 alongside Loch Lomond, then turn left onto the A83 which you follow through Arrochar, Inverary, Lochgilphead and Tarbert, all the way to Tayinloan and the signs for Gigha Ferry.

Facilities

You won't find any large supermarkets on the main road from Glasgow, but there are medium-sized stores for basic supplies in Inverary, Lochgilphead and Tarbert.

1.0 Gigha Ferry slipway

People crossed the Sound of Gigha, the very waters you are about to kayak, five thousand years ago. They had no GPS, VHF radios, flares or modern protective clothing. Tide tables were unheard of. Instead they lived their lives according to the rise and fall of the sea, and the movement of the sun and the moon. This is the rhythm you need to find. It has probably taken months of planning for you to reach the start of the trail, so savour this moment. Relax into the knowledge you are no longer completely in charge. You must work with your natural partners, the sea and the weather, because even if you throw a hissy-fit, you will not persuade either of them to change their mood.

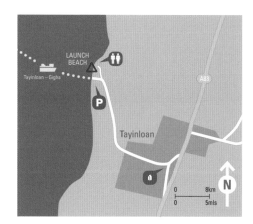

They may allow you to complete the trail or they may not, and this you must accept. More likely, they'll throw up a few obstacles, and when you successfully negotiate these, your satisfaction will be all the greater.

The Scottish Sea Kayak Trail doesn't actually start on the Isle of Gigha, the most southerly of the Hebridean Islands, but at the tiny mainland ferry port opposite. There's a hotel in the nearby village of Tayinloan and a tiny shop. From here, signs point the way to the Gigha Ferry, operated by the ubiquitous Caledonian MacBrayne, Scotland's state-owned ferry company and known to everyone as CalMac. There's a free, long-stay car park at the ferry jetty where vehicles can be left. It is frequently busy, so please park with care. Immediately to the north of the CalMac jetty is a small beach where you launch. Tide and weather permitting, depart around lunchtime, aiming to spend the rest of the day and night exploring Gigha. If, during your first night camping, you discover you've forgotten a key item, you can easily return to the vehicle without a major detour. So pack the kayaks, launch, and revel in the satisfaction that you have begun the Scottish Sea Kayak Trail.

Additional information

The waters upon which you are about to embark have been instrumental in shaping Scotland. Saint Columba brought Christianity here in the 6th century and, with his followers, built timber chapels and crude stone cells along the shores of Argyll. Roads and railways did not diminish the importance of the sea as a highway, but instead connected the tourists with steamships. The Gulf Stream warms the climate and allows an abundance of crops to grow. In this place, the sea is everything, so treat it with respect and you will be fine.

1.1 To Gigha (5km)

Don't underestimate this short crossing. The shallow sea bed, funnelled wind and curious tidal patterns combine to make the Sound of Gigha a surprising challenge. The published times of the tidal streams are not completely reliable, probably because this area is affected by two nearby large bodies of water, the Atlantic Ocean and the Irish Sea, which move up and down the opposite sides of Ireland at different times. The effects of their variations are felt on the way to Gigha.

There's also the matter of the CalMac ferry, the first of many you will encounter during the course of this trail. Like it, you are headed into Ardminish Bay,

📷 Tayinloan store.

which is also the most popular mooring for yachts. To the south of the CalMac ferry landing, there's a small jetty used by tenders from the yachts. Alongside this is a small sandy beach, just in front of the excellent Boathouse Café and the best place to land. Check out www.gigha.org.uk for more information about the island.

Facilities

The Boathouse Café has a good reputation and now plans to open from April to September (01583 505123, boathouse-bar.com). The 'official' campsite on Gigha (£3 per person per night in 2009) is alongside the café where there are basic toilets, showers (£1 coin) and a washing machine. Camping here used to be free, but the cafe owners say they are putting the modest fees towards building a proper shower and toilet block. There's also the Gigha Hotel (01583 505254, wwwgigha.org.uk) and some B&Bs. Wild camp spots can be found in more remote parts of the island, but Gigha deserves exploration on foot, and the campsite is a good base. It's a short walk to the medium sized Gigha Stores (01583 505251, www.gighastores.co.uk) , which also serves as the post office.

Directions

Launch your kayaks from the rough sand beach between the CalMac slipway at Tayinloan and the old pier slightly to the north. Make a direct 5km crossing into centre of Ardminish Bay and land on the beach close to south jetty, not the CalMac jetty. Make sure that you keep well clear of the ferry.

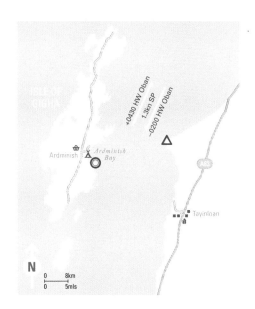

Sound of Gigha
N stream starts +0430 HW Oban
S stream starts –0200 HW Oban
1.3kn springs. Tidal streams in this area should be treated as approximations and calculations adjusted according to the evidence of your own eyes.

Additional information

Gigha is pronounced 'Geeya' and all the tourist information will tell you the name means 'God's Island'. This sounds nicer than simply, 'Good Island', or 'Island of Creeks', both of which are alternative derivations from the Old Norse. What a name cannot convey is the almost tangible tranquillity of the place, a deep, spiritual calm that, even if you have had all sorts of hassles trying to get here, is sure to cause you to relax.

There's mystery here too. Follow the signs south, past the Gigha Hotel, then turn west uphill to track down the Ogham Stone. You will find this 7th century granite pillar standing among gorse bushes and now almost covered in lichen. Were you permitted to scrape this off, you would find an ancient form of

1.0
1.1
1.2
1.3
1.4
1.5
1.6

Celtic writing, after which the stone was named, but which as yet has not been fully translated.

Below lie the ruins of St Catan's Chapel, marked on the OS map as 'Church' in gothic script. In the coming days you will see many remains of early Christianity, so it's worth exploring these at the start of the trail.

Then on your way back, call into Achamore Gardens. It has a fifty acre display of rare tropical plants and trees, including palm lilies and flame trees. These were planted by Sir James Horlick, who made his money from the hot-drink Horlicks, and who bought Gigha in 1944. Entrance to the gardens is £4.

The earliest voyagers

The first inhabitants of Scotland would have been very familiar with the route of the Scottish Sea Kayak Trail. These were the Mesolithic people who arrived after the end of the last Ice Age and were nomads, shifting their camps with the seasons, eating what they could hunt or catch. The sea was a principle source of food, raw materials and means of transport.

This lifestyle meant they left few traces for archaeologists to find, unless they were lucky enough to unearth one of the middens, rubbish dumps, which are often preserved in caves or under a rock shelter. A superb example was found at Sand just north of Applecross in Section 4.

The Mesolithic people would have been part of a network moving along the coast in small boats, exchanging goods and raw materials with people in other settlements. Some of the tools found at the Applecross site were made of bloodstone from the Isle of Rum while other materials came from Staffin on Skye.

Gigha now belongs to the one hundred and thirty people who live there. They set up a Community Trust in 2001 and bought the island with four million pounds of lottery and taxpayers' money. They now produce some of their own electricity with three wind turbines on the south of the island, nicknamed Faith, Hope and Charity.

1.0
1.1
1.2
1.3
1.4
1.5
1.6

📷 *The view across to Jura.*

1.2 To Kilberry Head (27km)

Compared to the south of Gigha, where the warm waters of the Gulf Stream allow tropical plants to flourish, the north end of the island feels more like Scotland ought to. Once you round Ardminish Point you will find fewer yachts and any crowds disappear by the time you reach East Tarbert Bay. At the south end of the bay, not marked on the OS map, is Beathag's Well, from which a sailor should draw water and throw it in his direction of travel to ensure a fair wind. This is just one of the many myths and legends which swirl around Gigha. Incidentally, you will find many places called 'Tarbert' – it's an Old Norse word, signifying a place where a boat could be dragged across land as a short-cut to avoid a long or difficult sea-passage.

The Scottish Sea Kayak Trail now makes a 7km crossing back to the mainland to Ronachan Point, which means 'Place of Seals'. You will see lots of common seals and Atlantic grey seals on the trail, but around here you might also glimpse an otter.

Detours are good

We did not follow the trail we devised. Why? The answer is that we woke on Gigha to good weather and decided to kayak around to the west coast. Once we reached the tombolo beach that separates Eilean Garbh from the rest of the island, the calm sea invited us to kayak directly to Rubha Cruitiridh. This flexible approach is how I recommend you tackle the entire trail. The route I've described is the safest and most efficient for most weather conditions, but you should make your own discoveries.

A very large CalMac ferry to Islay leaves and enters West Loch Tarbert daily, so take care while crossing its mouth to Eilean Traighe. Until now the land has been relatively flat, the scenery dominated by the sea and sky, but ahead the first of the great forests of Argyll shapes the skyline. Also ahead lie a series of fractured headlands. Like long, withered fingers, these claw their way into the sea and each presents its own tidal challenges.

The first, Ardpatrick Point, sets the tone with no landing place for 2km, then two quiet bays Ceann an-t-Silein and Loch Stornoway. On the map, Rubha Cruitiridh looks like an impenetrable cliff but its red, sandstone defences are breached by small, sandy bays. The seabed is shallow close to the coast and even a low wind can produce choppy seas. Fortunately, there are several beaches onto which escape can be made, including Kilberry Bay, from which it's a short walk to visit Kilberry Castle.

Reception of broadcasts by, and transmissions to HM Coastguard, from handheld marine VHF radios are very limited in this area.

Alternatively, press on around Kilberry Point to the formal campsite Port Ban Caravan Park. These are the last amenities you will find for several days and, since you are about to enter strong tidal waters, you might want somewhere dry and flat to work out your timings.

Facilities

Port Ban Caravan Park (01880 770224, www.portban.com) has a café and a tiny shop, too small for a full re-supply but with enough for one night. If you are planning to stay at the site, kayak north past all the caravans and land in the last bay, immediately in front of the camping field that has its own facilities in temporary buildings.

1.0
1.1
1.2
1.3
1.4
1.5
1.6

Directions

Head around Ardminish Point and explore the quiet north end of Gigha. If possible, aim to start the 7km crossing from Rubh'a' Chairn Bhain, past the rocks of Gamhna Gigha to Ronachan Point in the final hour of the south-going tidal stream. It will push you slightly south, against your direction of travel, but it should mean the north-going stream is not too fast around Ardpatrick Point and it will continue to carry you north to Port Ban. If landing in Loch Stornoway, be aware the bay is fenced off from the minor road.

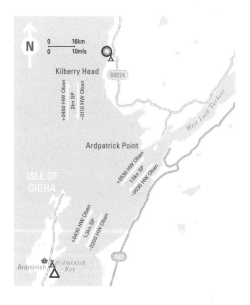

Entrance to West Loch Tarbert

In stream starts +0530 HW Oban

Out stream starts −0030 1.5kn at springs

Between Ardpatrick Point and Point of Knap

N stream starts +0450 HW Oban

S stream starts −0110 2kn at springs

Additional information

At the start of the Scottish Sea Kayak Trail, it's understandable if you want to keep going rather than make detours, particularly if they're on land. However, two historical sites are worth a mention. The first is a group of four thousand year old standing stones, the tallest of which is over three metres high, located just north of Balochroy. To visit, kayak from Gigha directly to them rather than to Ronachan Point. Of course, it would be easier drive here on your way to the start of the trail.

The second is Kilberry Castle, originally the home of the MacMhurrich clan, who were poets and harpists first, soldiers second. In the castle grounds there's an open display of mediaeval carved tombstones, remembering those who died in battle, the type of which is only found on Scotland's west coast.

1.3 To Carsaig Bay (33km)

As you have kayaked north, the panorama to the west has become dominated by the rugged Isle of Jura and its distinctive mountains, the 'paps'. The wedge-like shape of Jura, with Islay below, squeezes the tide on both flood and ebb. In this passage the full extent of its effects are felt. Some kayakers will relish the opportunity to play in the tide races and overfalls that lie ahead, but the route given here will enable you to encounter the least amount of moving water. Nevertheless, there will be some swiftly flowing sections, and if the wind is against the tide, it can be a rough ride with no convenient escape. For more detailed information consult the Sound of Jura chart or the other sources of information listed earlier. This and the next few passages present some of the most challenging tidal conditions on the whole of the Scottish Sea Kayak Trail.

From Port Ban, kayak up the coast to the spit of land at Eilean Traighe before crossing the mouth of Loch Caolisport, pronounced 'Killisport'. Tuck in behind Liath Eilein before completing the crossing and to study the conditions around the Point of Knap, where the spring tide runs at up to 1.5kn. Once around, pull into Kilmory Bay to wait for the tide and to decide whether or not to visit the MacCormick Islands, also called the MacCormaig Islands in some books.

Eilean Mor is well worth exploring, but the crossing should not be underestimated. When the tide is flowing strongly in either direction, significant tidal races of about 4 knots occur around these islands and become exceptionally serious when the wind blows against them. If you make this detour, consider it the crux of the day's passage and aim to cross and return at slack water.

Place names

The name of this country, 'Scotland', is derived from the Roman name for the inhabitants of Ireland. These people spoke the language we now call Gaelic and who travelled over to Scotland. Latin writers referred to these people as the 'Scoti'. They named the country 'Caledonia' after the mythical Greek hunting forest of Caledon. The natives of this new land were 'The Picts', a name which sometimes translates as 'The Painted People'.

Stay flexible

Having rounded Point of Knap against the south-going tide with few problems, we pulled into Kilmory Bay to snack and prepare for a crossing to Eilean Mor. The ebb tide was ending as we left Eilean nan Leac. Nevertheless, we found very lumpy water extending south from Corr Eilean as the slight tide was whipped up by a south westerly wind. We landed on and explored Eilean Mor, but when we hoped to leave six hours later, the wind had risen to the top end of force five. The sea between Eilean Mor and Corr Eilean was a boiling fury so we found a place to camp and departed the following morning on calm seas.

Reception of broadcasts by, and transmissions to HM Coastguard, from handheld marine VHF radios are very limited in this area.

Nowadays, places like Island of Danna and Rubha na Cille seem fantastically remote, at the very end of long, tiny roads. However, back in the days when the sea was the motorway and people travelled in small vessels, these were prime positions, so it's easy to understand why early Christian missionaries clustered around places like this. Our notions of accessibility have changed as our primary transportation has switched from boats to cars, yet these places still retain a special quality that we kayakers are lucky enough to experience.

If you left the MacCormick Islands at slack water,

1.0
1.1
1.2
1.3
1.4
1.5
1.6

or kayaked past the Island of Danna at slack water, then you should make it around Rubha na Cille while it's still slack before heading into the Sound of Jura. There are occasional places to land, but with no roads on this side of the peninsula it is a wild, wild coast until you reach Carsaig Bay. This is a superb sea kayaking area, offering the sort of experience that makes Scotland's west coast world-famous.

Facilities

There are no camping spots in Carsaig village but if you need to re-supply, locked kayaks could be safely left unattended here while you walk 1km over a slight rise to Tayvallich (www.tayvallich.com). It is a popular harbour for yachts, where you will find the Tayvallich Inn (01546 870282, www.tayvallich-inn.com) and a small store that's open Thursday to Saturday (01546 870281).

Directions

From Port Ban, follow the coast to Eilean Traighe and cross to behind Liath Eilein. At springs, a tide of up to 1.5kn runs off Point of Knap but it can be eddy-hopped at neaps and close to slack water. The area between Point of Knap and Rubha na Cille, the thin sliver of land north of the Island of Danna, is where the tidal streams are strongest. For example, they can run at 3.5kn between Eilean Ghamhna and the Island of Danna, and 3kn off Rubha na Cille. Aim to pass through here at slack water. If you are early, Kilmory Bay has a good beach on which to wait. Eilean Mor in the MacCormick Islands is a highly recommended detour in good weather. However,

fast tidal streams set up large eddies with overfalls and races, which become particularly fierce when the wind blows against tide. As such, it is easy to become stuck on the islands. Plan any visit to arrive and depart at slack water.

Ideally you will travel through this area as the south-going stream turns to north and then ride the flood tide up the Sound of Jura where several bays offer wild camping spots. However, if a significant wind is blowing from the north, this could mean you are heading into increasingly rough seas as the wind opposes the accelerating tide. If faced with such wind-over-tide, consider passing at the other slack, as north-going turns to south. With wind and tide against you, you will probably have to land and rest soon after completing the passage.

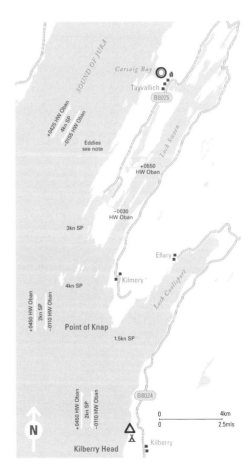

Tidal eddies run across Carsaig Bay and a reef extends south from the northern end, so there can be some turbulence as you enter.

In an emergency, you could avoid some of the tidal water by heading into Loch Sween and cutting behind Island of Danna, a passage only clear at high water. You would still have to round Rubha na Cille.

Between Point of Knap and Rubha na Cille

N stream starts +0450 HW Oban
S stream starts –0110 HW Oban

Off Point of Knap

1.5kn springs

Between MacCormick Islands and the mainland

3.5kn springs

Off Rubha na Cille

3kn springs

Among MacCormaig Islands

4kn springs

Between Rubha na Cille and Carsaig Bay

N stream starts +0425 HW Oban
S stream starts –0155 4kn springs. However, there are eddies nearly everywhere close to land and tidal streams along the coast set nearly one hour before those out in the channel.

Entrance to Loch Sween (detour)

In stream starts +0550 HW Oban
Out stream starts –0030 1.5kn springs

Additional information

Those early Christians knew a good spot when they found one. At Kilmory there are the remains of a 13th-century chapel while at Keills there's a 12th-century church, now renovated, open to the public and providing shelter to funeral slabs.

It was at Keills, just five hundred years after Christ, that St Cormac from Ireland founded his monastery. He really must have been a loner because, when the monastic life became too much of a rat-race for him, he'd head out to Eilean Mor among the MacCormick Islands and live in what all the guidebooks call 'a cave'. It's not a cave, that's far too glamorous a description. It's a vertical slot in a rocky cliff that is almost completely open to rain. It must have been a cold, wet, miserable retreat – all the better to punish Cormac's mortal flesh and contemplate God. Take a tent.

Apparently some early crosses are carved inside the cave on the east wall, but you may not be able to get out should you climb down to investigate.

In mediaeval times, the cave itself became a place of pilgrimage and a small chapel was built immediately in front of it, the remains of which are still standing. Then in the 13th century a much larger chapel was built in the centre of the island, and some time later a large cross was erected on the highest point. The original is now in the National Museum of Antiquities in Edinburgh, while the one that stands on the island is a replica.

📷 *The replica cross on Eilean Mor in the MacCormick Islands.*

1.0
1.1
1.2
1.3
1.4
1.5
1.6

🐦 Dalriada

There is some debate whether Gaelic evolved in Argyll and Ireland at the same time or whether it was brought over the sea from Ireland, and if so, who brought it.

The Scoti founded a kingdom called 'Dalriada' which, archaeological evidence suggests, was centred on Dunadd near Lochgilphead. The Scoti initially allied themselves with the native Picts to fight the Romans and, when the invaders withdrew in 410AD, Scoti and Picts turned on each other instead.

The Dalridic Kings consolidated their base in the area known today as Argyll, helped in 498AD when reinforcements arrived from Ireland led by three brothers. One of them was named Loarn and he took charge of the north of the Kingdom. To this day the area still bears his name, if not with its original spelling, and the water between Oban and Mull is called the Firth of Lorn.

Columba (Saint Columba as he became) landed in Dalriada in 563AD. Contemporary accounts describe a man of outstanding intelligence and eloquence. He first tried to convert Bruidhe, King of the Picts, then in 574 came back to bless Aidan, King of Dalriada. This didn't stop the fighting. Picts, Scoti, early Britons and Irish Picts all continued to fight with each other until collectively they faced a more formidable threat around 780AD – the Vikings.

1.4 To Crinan (10km)

This is a relatively short and simple passage, which can be combined with the previous or next passage to help hit times for slack water at key points. From Carsaig, cut behind Carsaig Island, where yachts often shelter, before following the densely wooded coast. There are no obvious exits until after you round Ardnoe Point and pull into the village of Crinan.

In summer this can be a very busy little village. Tourists come for a day out to watch the boats pass through the Crinan Canal, a 14.5km short-cut that avoids the Mull of Kintyre. You can kayak around to it and land on a slipway at high water, but it's a busy place and small boats might not be welcome.

A better alternative is to kayak into Crinan Harbour. The land south of Eilean da Mheinn dries out, so at low tide come around the north of the island.

📷 The first (or last) lock on the Crinan canal.

Facilities

There are no facilities and no shop in this part of Crinan, so you have to slog up-hill along the road, turn left, and then down hill again – about ten minutes in all. You first reach Crinan Boatyard, which has a very well-stocked chandlery that doubles as a tiny shop selling fresh milk and enough supplies for one night (01546 830232, www.crinanboatyard.co.uk). It is followed by the imposing Crinan Hotel (01546 830261, www.crinanhotel.com, a rather well-heeled place, where dinner, bed and breakfast costs over £100 per person in a magnificent location. If you plan a luxury blow-out, you could probably arrange to land at the boatyard's own slipway and store your kayaks there. Down by the canal itself is a small tea shop, run by the hotel, which sells sandwiches, cakes and drinks and is open 10am – 5pm during summer season.

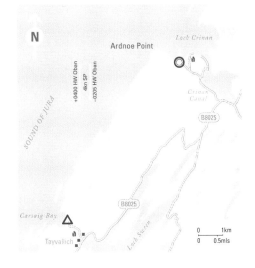

Between Ruadh Sgeir and the mainland

N stream starts +0400 HW Oban
S stream starts –0205 4kn springs

Additional information

Although it never flourished into anything more than a village, Crinan has long been a maritime crossroads. In the Bronze Age, people raised cattle here. In 574, St Columba landed nearby to bless Aidan as Scotland's first Christian King and it was from Crinan in 1819, at the start of the Clearances, that 525 Scots were herded onto ships bound for North America.

1.0
1.1
1.2
1.3
1.4
1.5
1.6

 ## Tidal tangle

We found tidal streams behaved strangely in the Sound of Jura. Expecting to have to paddle against a 1kn tide, we seemed to get a push, even when there wasn't much wind. I checked my calculations several times. I even checked the tide tables were accurate. I could not fully explain this, but when I checked the Admiralty Sailing Directions, I found the following advice, "The streams close inshore … begin to set 1 hour earlier than those in mid-channel." This explained our experience.

The Vikings

The first Viking attacks caused great confusion in the Kingdom of Dalriada. They had spent years fighting their regular enemies, the Picts, but these merciless men in their powerful sea-going vessels were strange and terrifying.

In 806AD, the Norse killed sixty-eight monks on Iona. Year after year they returned, plundered and murdered. In 839AD, the Picts took on the Norse and lost heavily. Almost all of the Picts' Royal line was wiped out. The Dalridic and Pictish Kingdoms merged, although in effect it was a take-over, as the customs, language and laws of the Picts were lost.

The Gaelic leader Kenneth MacAlpin became the first ruler of the kingdom called Alba in 843AD, making him the first King of Scotland. The centre of power moved from the west coast towards the centre of the country, leaving the coast clear for the Norsemen. Their invasion and colonisation began in 854AD.

The Crinan Canal opened in 1809, after taking decades to complete and requiring a tortuous route to avoid the unstable Crinan Moss. Within seven years it was shut, and Thomas Telford was called in to make repairs. Once operating normally, the canal allowed the Clyde herring fleet easy access to the shoals off the west coast. It also became popular with tourists who now had a fast route to the spectacular scenery of Scotland's west coast. Until the arrival of the motorcar and modern roads, it was one of the main routes north. The fastest way to travel from Glasgow to Inverness was by steamship, through the Crinan Canal, up the west coast to Fort William, and then through the Caledonian Canal. Even today, the Crinan Canal is used by more than two thousand vessels a year.

1.5 To Clachan Bridge (31km)

This passage takes you through some notoriously tricky waters but, with accurate tidal planning, these can be among the most enjoyable of the trail. Leave Crinan through the forest of yacht masts and cross the head of the loch to a sandy bay behind Rubha Garh-ard. This quiet bay is quite a contrast to the busy village opposite. 3km north-west lies a stretch of water marked on the map as the Dorus Mor, Gaelic for 'Great Door' or 'Gate'. The tide is squeezed between Craignish Point, on the mainland, and the island of Garbh Reisa, causing it to spurt out. In the Dorus Mor, that spurt runs at up to 8 knots at springs, that's almost 16km per hour.

Unless you are seeking excitement, you should ideally pass through here at slack water, as the north-going tidal stream is beginning. However, calculating slack water is not so simple, as the tide seems to have a mind of its own. The advice from a local guide is to pass through the centre of the channel, staying wide from the Garbh Reisa shore, or a large eddy may grab you and take you back around the island for a second attempt. Worse, you might be propelled in the direction of the whirlpool in the Gulf of Corryvreckan, although this is unlikely. If the wind is blowing against the tide, and you don't want to tackle rough water, consider seriously taking a day out. The Dorus Mor has claimed the lives of unprepared kayakers, so treat it with great respect.

Once through, if you need a rest, duck into sheltered Loch Beag at the head of which you will find Craignish Castle, built in the 12th or 13th century on the site of an earlier fortification which was probably constructed to repel Viking invaders. Work your way along the coast to Bagh Dail nan Cearn, then swing north towards Shuna Sound. The north-going stream should be helping now, as you pass between the islands of Shuna and Luing, the south end of which is spectacularly isolated. The Scottish Sea Kayak Trail takes the 'inside passage' through these waters, an easier route in rough weather. More adventurous kayakers with time to spare will find superb paddling on the west side of Luing, perhaps venturing through another tide-race at the northern end of Scarba, known as the 'Grey Dogs', and even out to the beautiful Garvellach Islands.

Our trail continues up the east coast of Torsa and through Seil Sound. Seil is a populated island where you are more likely to find a guest house than a wild camping spot. Balvicar has a working harbour, so take care on approach and land to the east of the high stone pier.

Seil Sound narrows dramatically at its northern end and becomes the Clachan Sound which dries completely. It's reported that, in the 1700s, for payment of a penny, a woman called Annie Bridges would carry visitors 'piggy-back' across the mud at low water. She was put out of business in 1791 when the Clachan Bridge was built.

The Clachan Bridge was later marketed to growing numbers of tourists as the 'Bridge over the Atlantic'. This was good business for Easdale, further down Seil Island, and also the Tigh-an-Truish Inn (01852 300242, www.tigh-an-truish.co.uk), Gaelic for the 'Inn of the Trousers' (see Additional information). There are no camping spots at the Clachan Bridge.

Facilities

A short walk takes you to the small–medium Balvicar Stores that boasts food, a wide range of beers and wines, and fresh bread daily (01852 300373, www.balvicarstors.co.uk). If it's necessary to leave the trail, there's a daily bus service to Oban operated by West Coast Motors.

Clachan Bridge, the bridge over the Atlantic.

 Dry & Wet

We approached the Clachan Bridge against a south-going stream and with the tide dropping fast. We knew we would have to portage, but didn't know how far or how many times. There were three sections, one before the bridge and two after, where we got out and either floated or dragged the boats, getting very wet feet in the process. I was all for spending the afternoon in the pub waiting for the tide to rise, but Liz insisted we press on.

1.0
1.1
1.2
1.3
1.4
1.5
1.6

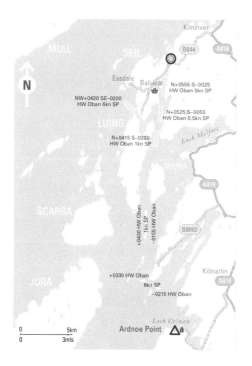

N

NW+0420 SE−0200
HW Oban 6kn SP

N+0555 S−0025
HW Oban 5kn SP

N+0525 S−0055
HW Oban 0.5kn SP

N+0415 S−0200
HW Oban 1kn SP

+0430 HW Oban
1kn SP
−0155 HW Oban

B8002

+0330 HW Oban
8kn SP
−0215 HW Oban

Kilninver

Easdale Balvicar

Loch Melfort

Kilmartin

Loch Crinan

Ardnoe Point

0   5km
0   3mls

Directions

From Crinan, cross Loch Crinan, keeping a careful watch for vessels heading to and from the canal and harbour entrances. Consider waiting on the beach behind Rubha Garh-ard for tide and weather to be in your favour. Unless you plan to tackle rough water and have the skills to cope, time your passage through the Dorus Mor when there is no wind against tide, and at slack water, ideally as the south-going stream turns north. Plan to leave the beach about an hour and a half before slack water in the Dorus Mor. As you cross between the islands of Liath-sgeir Mhor and Garbh Reisa, carefully watch the water ahead and judge whether it's flowing south or north. If it's still heading strongly south, understand that predicting slack water here is not a precise science, and tuck your kayaks into a pool of slack water close to Garbh Reisa.

The time to leave this spot is when you can break back into the flow and not be whisked south. Ensure you swing wide and choose a line near the centre

of the channel to avoid the eddy looping back around Garbh Reisa. If the wind is against even a slight tide, try to paddle against the end of the south-going stream and anticipate a rough ride.

Follow the coast and, when ready, head across to the gap between the ends of Luing and Shuna, riding the north-going tidal stream. The Scottish Sea Kayak Trail follows Shuna Sound (when working out tidal streams, don't confuse it with the Sound of Shuna, further north), passes the east side of Torsa and then Seil Sound which narrows dramatically at the Clachan Bridge. Progress past this point is impossible without several portages at low water as the Clachan Sound dries, so again careful timing is required.

Detour

Adventurous kayakers may detour to the Garvellachs or up the Sound of Luing, but be aware of the numerous, strong tidal streams in this area, all of which need careful calculation. This is particularly the case in the passage between Scarba and Lunga and around the island of Belnahua.

You can use the tidal stream information below to cut though the Cuan Sound and kayak the west side of Seil island. You will see more of the slate industry which once dominated this area, as well as the more remote side of Seil. However, if you have kayaked here directly from the Dorus Mor, the chances are the Cuan Sound will be in full flood and there might be significant overfalls at the exit.

Dorus Mor

W stream starts +0330 HW Oban
E stream starts −0215 8kn springs

Shuna Sound

N stream starts +0430 HW Oban
S stream starts −0155 1kn springs

East of Torsa
N stream starts +0415 HW Oban
S stream starts –0200 1kn springs

Seil Sound
N stream starts +0525 HW Oban
S stream starts –0055 0.5kn springs

Clachan Sound at the bridge
N stream starts +0555 HW Oban
S stream starts –0025 5kn springs

Cuan Sound (alternative route around Seil)
N stream starts +0420 HW Oban
S stream starts –0200 6kn at springs

Additional information

Luing, Seil and the other islands around here were once internationally famous and known generally as 'The Slate Islands'. The small village of Balvicar was developed as a slate quarrying port and, if you call in at the shop, you will walk past workers' cottages built in the 19th century.

Most of the industrial heritage lies off the Scottish Sea Kayak Trail on the more exposed west coast. It is centred on the island of Easdale, from where slate was taken to roof many of Scotland's great buildings, including cathedrals in Glasgow and Paisley. By 1860, more than nine million slates were exported each year around the world and more than four hundred and fifty people lived and worked on tiny Easdale Island, which is less than a mile across.

Gunpowder led to even deeper excavation and pits reached 80m below sea level. Then in November 1881, the main quarry was flooded when a ferocious storm breached the thin walls, the spot where the sea burst through still visible to this day. (www.easdale.org)

Further north, an entertaining story is told about the naming of the Tigh-an-Truish Inn, Gaelic for the 'Inn of the Trousers'. After the failed Jacobite rebellion of 1745, the wearing of any form of highland dress was outlawed. However, so the story goes, the people of Seil ignored this law and, if they had to visit the mainland, would borrow a pair of trousers from the inn before fording Clachan Sound, changing back on their return. It's a great story, but the present owner believes it to be complete fiction. It's more likely her Inn is named after a tailor who used to live alongside as the census return of 1791 records a family of trouser-makers alongside the present complex of buildings.

Inn of the Trousers.

1.6 To Oban (18km)

The Clachan Sound feels more like a river than the sea, yet it changes direction every six hours, and flows at 5 knots during spring tides, so you have to catch it heading north. You emerge among some lovely islands where you are almost certain to find a flotilla of yachts. Puilladobhrain (pronounced 'Pul-dorhan') is one of the most popular anchorages on the west coast.

After all the excitement of strong tidal streams, the rest of this passage may seem relatively tame but it will allow you the freedom to concentrate less on timings and more on the scenery. It also gives you time to think how you will plan the shuttle back to the car and whether you will overnight in Oban or camp before you get there.

The passage is sheltered significantly by the Isle of Mull, yet the coast is rugged with no exits until you reach Barrnacarry Bay. This is a lovely spot to spend some time if you need to work out what to do next. If time is short, you can make a dash for Oban but the trail would not be complete unless it visited the south end of the lovely island of Kerrera.

Either cross directly from Barrnacarry Bay to Rubha Seanach or go via the cliffs of Minard Point, then round the corner into Port a'Chroinn. From the sea, gaze up to the imposing form of Gylen Castle, one of many fortifications that are the dominant feature of the Section 2 of this trail. At low tide, it is very difficult to land and secure the boats on either this rocky beach or its neighbour Port a'Chaisteil, but if you manage a landing, climb up to the ruins. In good weather you will be rewarded with a stunning panorama encompassing much of the first section of this trail.

Facilities

If you land on the south end of Kerrera you will be close to a bed for the night at the Kerrera Bunkhouse and tea shop, which is in open Wednesday – Sunday at Lower Gylen (01631 570223, www.kerrerabunkhouse.co.uk). If you want to visit Gylen Castle or stay at the bunkhouse, but find you cannot land and unload boats on the rocky beaches, kayak back around Rubha Seanach and up the Sound of Kerrera, to a bay called 'The Little Horse Shoe'. From here it's less than two kilometres to the bunkhouse.

Because so many vessels, large and small, pass through relatively confined stretches of water, there is a voluntary code for safe navigation in the approaches to Oban, details of which can be found

1.0
1.1
1.2
1.3
1.4
1.5
1.6

Tricky landing but a great view of Gylen Castle.

in the Admiralty Pilot. Keeping close to the Kerrera shore, which is the most attractive, staying well out the way of the ferry that crosses to the mainland is recommended.

Although you have to keep your wits about you, the final passage up the Sound of Kerrera is easy, so you will probably allow your mind to drift back to the earlier, more challenging passages. The open seas around Gigha might be what you recall, or those long fractured headlands with their swift tides. Every day on this trail is utterly different to the last, presenting new challenges and fresh adventures. If you continue north, although it seems impossible to believe, the days just keep getting better.

Even if your journey doesn't end in Oban, you should take the time to shuttle your vehicle from the Gigha ferry. When you finally leave the trail, you will find that Oban is much easier to reach by public transport than Tayinloan. It's best to plan to spend at least one day in Oban, so where you land depends upon where you plan to spend the night.

Probably the easiest option is to cross from The Little Horse Shoe Bay on Kerrera to the mainland and land at Port nan Cuil, just before the Puffin Dive Centre. Leave the empty, locked kayaks in the bay, and walk a short distance up to the Gallanachmore Farm Campsite (☎ 01631 562425, www.obancaravanpark.com). Don't be dismayed by the caravans high on a hill, the camping field is closer to the water. There's a weekday bus service to Oban from the site, although on Saturdays you' will have to walk or take a taxi (about £7). The round trip shuttle to collect a car from the start can take about seven hours.

In bad weather or if you fancy a bed for the night, you could book into one of the hotels, Guest Houses or the Scottish Youth Hostel (☎ 01631 562025, www.syha.org.uk) which line the esplanade at the north end of the bay. You don't have to be a member to use the hostel and, if you ask nicely, the manager will allow you to leave kayaks around the back of the building near the bike shed. If you choose to overnight on the town, this is the way to approach it. Stay on the Kerrera shore, cross Ardantrive Bay to the north-east corner of the island and, after checking no vessel is entering or leaving the north channel, cross directly to the mainland at its narrowest point. In front of the promenade wall is a patch of shingle beach called the Corran Ledge with a slipway behind. It is almost opposite the Scottish Youth Hostel, which is marked on the OS map with a red triangle.

If you are leaving the Scottish Sea Kayak Trail in Oban, then draw satisfaction from knowing you have completed one of the most technical sections to kayak, and remember, there are another three sections just waiting for you to try. If you are continuing from Oban, then count your blessings.

Directions

Leave the Clachan Bridge on the north-going tidal stream as soon as the water in the Clachan Sound is deep enough to pass. Follow the coast to Barrnacarry Bay, cross to Minard Point, then cross the Sound of Kerrera to Rubha Seanach and pull into Port a'Chroinn to take a look at Gylen Castle. Dramatic fortifications perched on headlands are a feature of this area and Gylen is one of the most impressive. Return to Sound of Kerrera and follow the island shore. If camping, cross from The Little Horse Shoe Bay to Port nan Cuil, land and walk to campsite. If heading for the town, continue north past Ardantrive Bay. Provided the north channel is clear of vessels, cut directly across to mainland, and kayak back towards Oban, aiming to land close to one of the slipways near the Scottish Youth Hostel, marked on the OS map with a red triangle, in front of which there is free long-stay car parking.

1.0
1.1
1.2
1.3
1.4
1.5
1.6

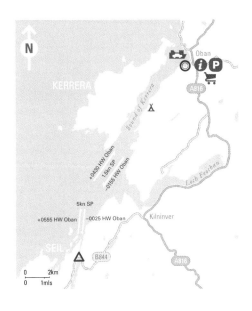

1.0
1.1
1.2
1.3
1.4
1.5
1.6

Clachan Sound at the bridge

N stream starts +0555 HW Oban

S stream starts −0025 5kn springs

Sound of Kerrera

NE stream starts +0430 HW Oban

SW stream starts −0155

1.5kn where wider, 2kn where narrow at springs

Additional information

The island of Kerrera forms a huge natural break-water and is what makes Oban such a good harbour. Only around thirty people live on the island, so it is quiet, peaceful and a world apart from the bustle of the tourist centre it overlooks.

Gylen Castle was built in 1582 by the Clan MacDou-gall but was occupied for a relatively short period of time. It was burnt to the ground by General Leslie during the Wars of the Three Kingdoms, which sounds like something written by J.R.R. Tolkien, but was actually a religious-based civil war which engulfed Scotland, Ireland and England in the 17th century. The Covenanter army of Scotland, com-manded by Leslie, fought alongside the English Parliamentary army against the forces of the King. It was during the burning of Gylen Castle that the famous Brooch of Lorn disappeared and remained lost for 180 years. It had belonged to King Robert the Bruce who, in 1306, had travelled the land trying to unify his Kingdom. He was ambushed and, so the story goes, the famous brooch that had held fast his cloak was torn away in battle. It was found in the mud still clutched by the severed hand of a MacDougall. The MacDougall clan kept the brooch at Gylen but after castle was ransacked, it disap-peared for almost two centuries. When it eventually reappeared, it was returned to the MacDougalls who now keep it safe. Meanwhile, extensive reno-vation work has been carried out at Gylen Castle and since 2006 visitors have been able to go inside the building.

If you have time to spare, then a circumnavigation of Kerrera is a great day's kayaking, and you might consider wild camping on the more remote west coast. However, be warned – the west coast has such breath taking views across to Mull and Mor-vern, you are guaranteed to be tempted to tackle the second section of the Scottish Sea Kayak Trail.

Shuttle information

If you plan to tackle Section 2 of the Scottish Sea Kayak Trail, you might want to leave the car at the Gigha ferry until you reach Mallaig. This is a valid option, particularly if you are enjoying a run of good weather, but the shuttle from Mallaig can only just be done in a day, as it requires a train and three buses to get back to Tayinloan. Also finding some-where to store the kayaks in Mallaig, while you make the journey, is tricky. Furthermore, if bad weather prevents you from rounding Ardnamurchan Point you might need to drive yourselves and your kayaks further up the trail, and you will find retrieving the car much easier from Oban than Tayinloan.

Learn the etiquette of driving on single-track roads. Passing places are provided every few hundred yards and these should be used to allow oncoming traffic to pass. Indicate and pull in on your side of the road, even if the passing place is on the other side, then wave as the car passes. If you see a vehicle coming up fast behind you, or clearly trying to pass, the same rule applies. Locals get frustrated with visitors who ignore the signs saying 'Use passing places to permit overtaking'.

If you see sheep, slow down. They are kamikaze menaces whose sole aim in life is to leap in front of your vehicle and test the strength of your bumper bar. If you hit one, you are obliged to inform the police.

So for all these reasons, if you are continuing on the trail, it is recommended you move your vehicle to Oban and leave it in the on-street, long-stay car parking area along the esplanade from the Scottish Youth Hostel.

Timetables and service numbers change from year to year, so check transport arrangements for yourself. Traveline Scotland has details of almost every bus, rail and ferry service (0871 200 2233, www.travelinescotland.com) but treat it with caution as its website sometimes recommends crazy routes.

Oban – Lochgilphead: The bus stops are arranged in a small crescent immediately in front of the railway station and pedestrianised harbour area of Oban town centre. Those heading north are on one side, south on the other, and you want the side furthest from the sea. Catch the south-bound 423 service operated by West Coast Motors. There are four buses Monday – Friday, two on Saturday and none on Sunday. The 09:15 reaches Lochgilphead at 10:33.

Lochgilphead – Tayinloan Village: It's the same Lochnell Street stop for both buses. Service 926 operated by Citylink Coaches or West Coast Motors departs at 11:35 and arrives in Tayinloan at 12:45.

Tayinloan Village – Ferry terminal: You will have to walk the remaining 1km to the car at the ferry terminal, because few buses go down this small road.

Gigha Ferry slipway – Oban: You will now appreciate, only too well, that the roads around here do not allow speedy travel. Follow the A83 to Lochgilphead. It turns right into the town, but you continue straight ahead onto the even slower A816. Once you reach Oban, if you are heading for the campsite, then Gallanachmore is signposted from the roundabout in the centre of the town. If you are heading for the youth hostel, follow signs to the A85 until you reach the sea front and follow the promenade to the hostel.

1.0
1.1
1.2
1.3
1.4
1.5
1.6

Looking back to Kerrera from Port nan Cuil.

BUSINESS HOURS

OPEN Most days About 9 or 10
Occasionally as Early as 7, But SOME DAYS
As Late As 12 or 1.
WE CLOSE About 5:30 or 6
Occasionally About 4 or 5, But
Sometimes as Late as 11 or 12.
SOME DAYS OR Afternoons, WE
Aren't Here At All, and Lately
I've Been Here Just About All the Time,
Except When I'm Someplace Else,
But I Should Be Here Then, Too.

A sign in the window of Gigha Stores, page 65.

The Ogham Stone (page 65).

The Crinan canal, a shorcut to the Firth of Clyde (page 72).

Landing and camp next to the Boathouse Café (page 65).

An Old Clyde 'puffer' livng up to its name.

📷 *Deep water in the Sound of Mull, which reaches depths of 150m (page 94).*

Oban harbour (page 85).

Stranded in Loch Sunart (page 96).

Mull railway (page 86).

Crenellated aid to navigation, approaching Duart Point (page 88).

A shell beach in Loch Moidart (page 103).

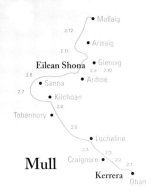

2.12
Mallaig
2.11
Arisaig
Eilean Shona
Glenuig
2.9 2.10
2.8
Ardtoe
Sanna
2.7
Kilchoan
2.6
Tobermory
2.5
Lochaline
2.4
2.3
Mull
Craignure
2.2
2.1
Kerrera
Oban

Lords of the Isles

Section 2: Oban – Mallaig 150km

This section of the Scottish Sea Kayak Trail will take you to three of the largest towns on the west coast and through some of the region's busiest waters. Yet this stretch also contains Ardnamurchan Point, the most remote and challenging headland yet to be encountered on the trail. The coastline is dotted with castles, some ruined, some still occupied. These are the legacy from a bloody history of feuding clans, savage clearances and the Lords of the Isles. Despite the exposure on the headlands and the strong tidal streams around Lady's Rock, this is the easiest of the long sections on this trail.

OS Sheets:
49, 47 & 40
Tide tables:
Oban & Ullapool

Travel to the start

A bustling port, railway terminus, coach depot and excellent communications make the tourist town of Oban in Argyll the logical place to begin Section 2 of the trail. It is only a two-hour drive from Glasgow. To reach it, follow the A82 up the side of Loch Lomond to Tyndrum, then take the A85 to Oban.

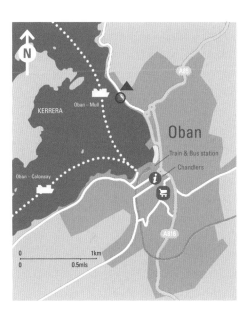

KERRERA
Oban – Mull
Oban
Train & Bus station
Chandlers
Oban – Colonsay
0   1km
0   0.5mls
N
A85
A816

2.0 Oban

From the shelter of Oban Bay, it's easy to under-estimate the crossing to Mull. Firstly, these are very busy waters, with everything from rowing boats to ferries and vast cargo ships crossing your path. You should wear bright coloured clothing and have the VHF handy when leaving Oban.

Secondly, there are significant tidal effects in the Firth of Lorn. The north-going flood tide divides into at least three streams off the south end of Lismore. On the south-going ebb, the waters meet in roughly the same place, so in either direction the water is disturbed.

Thirdly, the weather outside Oban Bay can be very different to the weather inside. The island of Kerrera forms a natural breakwater, so once you have made it around the northern tip, it's worth re-assessing conditions and adjusting timings if necessary. If a north wind is blowing, wait until you are well out of the bay before making that assess-ment, as the exit from Oban harbour is hit by winds travelling the full fetch of the Sound of Mull.

To reach the water, head to the north of the town and the long promenade in front of the Scottish

2.0
2.1
2.2
2.3
2.4
2.5
2.6
2.7
2.8
2.9
2.10
2.11
2.12

Youth Hostel and other hotels. Several concrete slipways lead down onto a shingled beach, marked on the map as the Corran Ledge, where Section 2 of the trail begins.

SYHA Oban.

Facilities

You will find four large supermarkets, Tesco, Co-op, Lidl and Aldi, near the town centre. There's a chandlers on the high street, Nancy Black (01631 562550), and a specialist kayak shop, Sea Kayak Oban (01631 565310, www.seakayakoban. com) as well as Outside Edge, an outdoor equipment shop that sells kayaking gear (01631 566617, www.outsideedgeoban. com). Oban specialises in sea food, with up-market restaurants and take-away fish and chip shops. The Tourist Information Centre will advise on accommodation, which is plentiful and to suit all pockets. The Scottish Youth Hostel (01631 562025, www.syha.org.uk) is on the esplanade at the north end of the bay alongside several hotels and guest houses. There is free, long-stay, on-street parking in front of these establishments where you can leave your vehicle while kayaking this section. Oban police say car crime is not a major problem in the town, and provided you park in a long-stay bay, you won't have to inform them where you are headed.

Additional information

The name Oban in Gaelic means 'Little Bay'. There's evidence the Vikings used it on their summer raids and, much later, it became a fishing station for the British Fisheries Society. However, it was tourism which made Oban a thriving town, particularly after the steamship *Comet* linked the town to Glasgow in 1812. Queen Victoria was among the visitors in 1847, calling Oban, "One of the finest spots we have seen", after which guidebooks placed it among the most fashionable of Scottish watering-places. The railway arrived in 1880 and with it, even more tourists, many of whom used it as the starting point for visits to Staffa.

Passengers can still catch ferries from here to Scotland's outer isles, adding to the tourists who continue to flock here during the summer months, making Oban one of the busiest towns on the west coast. It's worth bearing this in mind when planning accommodation.

2.1 To Kerrera (1.5km)

The rugged island of Kerrera is a peaceful contrast to busy Oban. Slatrach Bay on the north-west corner offers an easy landing if you want to explore the north of the island and wait for the correct tide time to start the crossing to Mull.

Directions

Leave the Corran Ledge following the curve of the harbour. When you are certain no traffic is using the channel, at the narrowest point, cross directly to north end of Kerrera where there is a large, concrete red and white hooped channel marker. Hug the Kerrera coast and make your way around the island to Rubh a' Bhearnaig.

North entrance to Oban Bay

N stream starts –0130 HW Oban

S stream starts +0455 2.5kn springs

Additional information

If you land and explore the island, you will find an obelisk on a hill overlooking the north channel. This is Hutcheson's Monument, erected to honour David Hutcheson, one of the founders of the ferry company which became Caledonian MacBrayne. Originally a private company, 'CalMac' is now state owned and, because no other company seems to want all the routes, has a virtual monopoly on services to the islands of the west coast. The locals have a love-hate relationship with this lifeline service and you may come to hear on your travels the rhyme: "To God belongs the earth, and all that it contains – except the Clyde and the Western Isles. They're Caledonian MacBrayne's". There are several variations, but the theme is the same.

Ⓞ The CalMac ferry enters the busy Oban harbour. Children under five travel free, pets are welcome and travel free. Bicycles, kayaks, canoes and surfboards all go free, subject to space, on all CalMac services.

2.2 To Duart Castle (12km)

This is a tricky crossing that requires precise planning based around the timing of tidal streams on the Mull shore. The two lighthouses off the end of Lismore become visible the moment you round the north tip of Kerrera. One appears as you might expect, the other is a four-sided pyramid tower with a red cap marking Lady's Rock.

The admiralty chart for the area shows a strong tidal race south of Lady's Rock and extensive overfalls between it and Lismore, and also between it and Mull. This is where the flood tide divides into three streams: one travels north up the Sound of Mull; one heads north-east into Loch Linnhe; and the last heads up the Lynn of Lorn. Conversely, this is where the ebb tides meet, and at full ebb, the tidal race runs hardest. When wind opposes tide, the overfalls and other features are at their worst. Indeed, the pilot warns that in such conditions this area is dangerous and should be avoided.

In calm conditions, or for those seeking rough water, a detour to Lady's Rock is interesting, but the Scottish Sea Kayak Trail steers clear of the liquid turmoil. It travels south down the west coast of Kerrera, makes a direct 6km crossing to Mull, then follows the coast north. Time your crossing to pass between Mull and Lady's Rock at slack water, preferably as the south-going ebb turns to north-going flood. This way, during the crossing from Kerrera, the ebb will have carried you away from trouble and, once successfully across, the flood will take you in the direction you wish to travel, northward into the Sound of Mull. Make sure not to go too

LORDS OF THE ISLES

2.0
2.1
2.2
2.3
2.4
2.5
2.6
2.7
2.8
2.9
2.10
2.11
2.12

early or pass too close to Lady's Rock, or the ebb overfalls will be a problem.

To add to the complications, slack water can be more of a theoretical concept than a practical reality in these waters. Shipping is also an added hazard. Huge cargo vessels head up and down Loch Linnhe carrying road stone from Glensanda quarry on Morvern, while CalMac ferries use this route into the Sound of Mull. There are numerous marinas in the area and yachts can be heading in almost any direction. Take your time, do your calculations and only leave Kerrera when you are satisfied that all is well.

If the wind is against tide, or the sea looks too rough, seriously consider the wisdom of attempting this crossing. Explore beautiful Kerrera until the sea calms down or head back to Oban. You can drive your kayaks to the CalMac terminal, re-park the car, and then carry the boats onto the ferry to Craignure on Mull.

Once across, head north along the Mull shore past a crenellated monument with its own turret, topped by a solar panel and navigation light, quite the most ornate shipping aid in the area. Here you turn into the Sound of Mull, skirt the base of Duart Castle, then curve back on yourself into Duart Bay. This is a shingle beach backed by a large grassy area, from which a path leads up to the castle itself. Duart Castle is a recommended stop, not only to experience its history, but also Mary's fruitcake.

Facilities

Tucked away at the back of the gift shop (01680 812309, www.duartcastle.co.uk) is an excellent café with home-made scones and cakes, internet access and friendly staff who are knowledgeable about the history of the clan Maclean, of which the castle is the clan seat. Entrance to the castle is £5.

 # Rough stuff

We struggled out of Oban north channel against a Force 5 wind rocketing down the Sound of Mull and across the Firth of Lorn. We had escaped its full effect when we reached Rubha na Lice on Kerrera and decided to make the crossing, hoping we would find shelter as we neared Mull. This proved very hard work, and there was no shelter until we were close enough to touch dry land.

Liz suggested camping but, with the promise of excellent home-made fruitcake in the tea-shop, I insisted on going around to Duart Bay. We passed the monument and turned left into the Sound of Mull, straight into a Force 6 head wind. We only just managed to make progress, battering into the gusts, crashing up and over the waves, and as we turned left again to head into the bay, the shoulder height waves were now breaking on our beam. These threatened to lift and dash us onto the castle rocks as if we were invaders. The big, stable P&H Cetus kayaks, heavily loaded, proved their worth, with Liz admitting later that she'd have capsized in her usual kayak.

We were still shaking when we landed on the beach and headed for the tea-shop. If anything, the experience improved our appetites.

Directions

From Slatrach Bay on Kerrera, head out to Rubha na Lice where there's a small shingle beach. Cross the Firth of Lorn heading for Grass Point and then follow the Mull coast north. Time your crossing to reach the area between Mull and Lady's Rock at slack water, ideally as the ebb turns to flood, five hours and forty-five minutes before high water at Oban. Then allow the north-going tidal stream to carry you into the Sound of Mull to Duart Point. You may encounter severe difficulties if the wind is blowing against the tide.

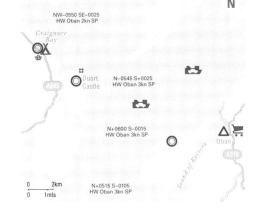

Firth of Lorn – south east of Loch Spelve on Mull

NE stream starts +0515 HW Oban
SW stream starts –0105 3kn springs

Off Grass Point on Mull

N stream starts +0600 HW Oban
S stream starts –0015 3kn springs

Between Mull and Lismore

N stream starts –0545 HW Oban
S stream starts +0025 3kn springs
4kn between Lady's Rock & Lismore
Expect overfalls if wind is against tide
On flood, there are eddies and severe turbulence
NW Lismore light

Sound of Mull – south east entrance

NW stream starts –0550 HW Oban
SE stream starts –0025 2kn springs

Additional information

Duart Castle has been the stronghold of the Clan Maclean since 1250. It never succumbed to an invading army but fell victim to politics after Hector Maclean supported the Jacobite cause and fought alongside Charles Edward Stuart, 'Bonnie Prince Charlie', at Culloden in 1746. The price of defeat was the confiscation of Duart Castle which was subsequently used to garrison the English troops of George 2nd until 1751. Outside the castle is a small graveyard where some of these soldiers and their families are buried. This patch of earth was consecrated by an English bishop so the dead would not have to lie in a 'heathen's graveyard'. Duart lay abandoned for many years until the 26th chief Sir Fitzroy Maclean bought and renovated it in 1911.

The lighthouse on Eilean Musdile, at the southern end of Lismore, was built by Alan Stevenson, a member of the celebrated family that built most of Scotland's lighthouses in seemingly impossible locations. Lime was quarried on the west coast of the island and, while it's not worth a detour, you can still see the kilns and quarrymen's cottages on Eilean nan Caorach at the north end.

Lady's Rock takes its name from yet another bloody event in Scottish history. Lady Elizabeth Campbell was abandoned here to drown by the man she was forced to marry, Lachlan Maclean of Duart Castle. Rescued, she fled to her father who said nothing when Lachlan turned up and claimed she had died of sickness. Instead a banquet was ordered for his grieving son-in-law. Imagine Lachlan's surprise when Lady Elizabeth showed up.

2.3 To Craignure (3.5km)

The tricky tidal planning is now over for a day or two and you are in the relatively sheltered waters of the Sound of Mull. Travelling from Duart Castle to Craignure is just a short hop across a bay but again, with all the marine traffic around, you will need your wits about you.

Facilities

Craignure is the largest of four ferry terminals on Mull (the others are at Fionnphort, Tobermory and Fishnish) and where the large car ferry disgorges its passengers. Should escape be necessary, CalMac allows kayaks to be carried onto the car deck of the ferry for the voyage back to Oban. Shieling Holidays campsite (01680 812496, www.shielingholidays. co.uk) has a landing beach just before the small jetty on the south of Craignure Bay and is a good option, with tent places, a hostel and 'shielings', curious semi-permanent tent-like structures which can be rented. The Craignure Inn is nearby (01680 812305, www.craignure-inn. co.uk) and a small steam train takes tourists south to another stately home and gardens. If you are just looking for a place to eat or re-supply, kayak to a

small shingle beach by another slipway on the north side of the CalMac terminal. From here you can walk back to the small–medium sized Craignure Stores (01680 812301), Tourist Information Centre (01680 812377), and MacGregor's Roadhouse (01680 812471) which serves hot meals all day and has internet access. At the north of the bay is the impressive Isle of Mull Hotel (0870 950 6267, www.crerarhotels.com).

Don't make the mistake two paddlers did when they kayaked from Glasgow to Skye in 1934. In his excellent book *The Canoe Boys*, Sir Alastair Dunnett describes how he and Seamus Adam came ashore after dark and set up their tent on a flat piece of lush grass, only to wake the following morning and find themselves camped on Scallastle golf course.

Directions

From Duart Bay, paddle up the coast towards Craignure and head for the small jetty on the south of the bay. Looking ahead, if time is short, the fastest way to Tobermory is to follow the Mull coast. There are also more hotels, guest houses and restaurants on this side of the Sound; however, the more interesting kayaking is to cross to Morvern.

All day food in Craignure.

**Sound of Mull –
south east entrance**
NW stream starts –0550 HW Oban
SE stream starts –0025 2kn springs

2.0
2.1
2.2
2.3
2.4
2.5
2.6
2.7
2.8
2.9
2.10
2.11
2.12

90

Dominus Insularum

The Norse controlled the west coast for four hundred years. The Outer Hebrides, which they controlled longer, were known as the Islands of the Foreigners. Although they left their mark on places names, they never completely overwhelmed the Gaelic culture.

The first effective rebel was Somerled, who curiously enough was part Gael, part Norse. He copied their design of longship and began a guerilla campaign to recover his family's lands in Morvern. After a series of ferocious land and sea battles, he triumphed over Godred the Black and by 1160 was King of Argyll and technically Lord of the Isles. However, it was not until 1336 the formal title 'Dominus Insularum' (Lord of the Isles) was first used by John of Islay.

John's death in battle just four years later saw the Lordship transfer to the Clan Donald, where it became forever associated with the Gaelic language, culture and a predilection to challenge the authority of the Scottish Crown. Until, that is, one of the Lords, John MacDonald, in 1462 signed a treaty with the English Crown. His son considered this a betrayal, and Angus Og defeated his father and his allies. However, the power to grant the title had shifted to the Crown rather than assumed by an independent prince. The eldest male child of the British monarch now takes the title Lord of the Isles.

2.4 To Lochaline (11km)

Crossing the Sound of Mull is the busiest stretch of the whole trail and the closest you will come to a marine motorway. Fortunately, nature has placed the equivalent of mini-roundabouts in a convenient line which can be used as stepping stones.

From Craignure, head to the skerry of Sgeir non Gobhar, then kayak on past the light on Glas Eileanan. Once you are level with Eilean Rubha an Ridire, you are safely through the large traffic. There are no roads to this remote corner of Morvern in contrast to busy Craignure. A wild place, there's a good chance of seeing golden or sea eagles.

 # Another diversion

Again we diverted from the trail. The wind was still blowing hard down the Sound of Mull, so not only would it have been difficult to cross to the Morvern shore, the topography meant we could find more shelter by ducking into the bays and behind the headlands on the Mull coast.

We followed this coast north until the ferry terminal at Fishnish where Allan serves excellent coffee and fish and chips in the Secret Kitchen café. We crossed to the Morvern shore at this point, missing Lochaline altogether.

A small sea can run off Ardtornish Point, where there's a ruined castle, then it's an easy kayak into Lochaline, pronounced 'LochAllan'. This is the only settlement of size on the Morvern shore.

Open shelter, Inninmore Bay.

Facilities

The small village has a tiny shop, not big enough for a full re-supply, as well as the Lochaline Hotel (01967 421657) and an up-market restaurant, The White House (01967 421777, thewhitehouserestaurant. co.uk). There's also a three-times a week bus service, operated by Shiel Buses and a little CalMac car ferry which makes regular crossings to Fishnish on Mull and will carry kayaks. Lochaline is a quiet place where, with care, it should be possible to leave secured kayaks safely overnight.

7km north of Lochaline is the small formal campsite at Fiunary with just twenty-five pitches (01967 421225).

Directions

Cross the Sound of Mull in the shortest distance, by kayaking from the relative safety of one skerry to the next. When you reach the remote Morvern shore, turn north-west and explore the coast which leads to Lochaline. Land either on the beach to the north-east of the Lochaline Hotel or head into the loch and land just north of the CalMac slipway.

Sound of Mull – south east entrance

NW stream starts –0550 HW Oban
SE stream starts –0025 2kn springs

Loch Aline entrance

In stream starts –0525 HW Oban
Out stream starts +0040 2.5kn springs

Lochaline Hotel.

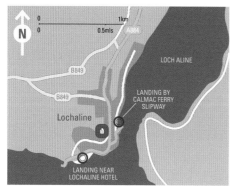

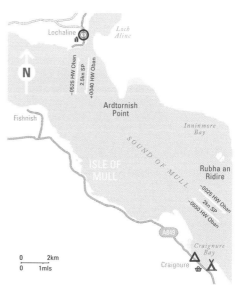

2.0
2.1
2.2
2.3
2.4
2.5
2.6
2.7
2.8
2.9
2.10
2.11
2.12

2.5 To Tobermory (22km)

If the wind is at your back and tide is with you, it's an easy paddle up the Sound of Mull. If they're against you, it's a slog. Just put your head down and crank out the miles, taking care to avoid the many ships that pass. After 14km, the Sound narrows at Dun Ban, and this is the place to cross to Rubh' an t-Sean Chaisteil.

📷 Tobermory, the 'capital' of Mull. Twice made famous by children's television.

Ahead you see Calve Island. It is a natural break-water sheltering Tobermory harbour in much the same way Kerrera shelters Oban. Calve is a lovely, quiet island, now inhabited only by sheep, except during occasional weeks when the farmhouse is used as a holiday cottage. The small island at its south end, Cnap a' Chailbhe, is almost attached, but Doirlion a' Chailbhe is a narrow channel between Calve and Mull and the best way to approach the town by kayak. If you are planning a short stay, and it's not high tide, land on the beach to the north-east (right) of the harbour wall. If that's covered, or if you're staying for longer, head to the slipway at the west end of the main street.

📷 Fish & chips on the quayside.

Facilities

Tobermory is a relatively large tourist town with a wide range of essentials for the itinerant sea kayaker. You will find a supermarket, chandlers and youth hostel, as well as countless places to eat and drink, all lined up along the brightly painted street that runs the length of the sea front. During a summer's day, there are enough tourists around to safely leave the kayaks for an hour or so while in search of food or re-supply. You will find one of Scotland's best fish and chip vans parked on the harbour wall. The nearest formal campsite is inconveniently uphill from the town.

There are no obvious places where you could safely leave a sea kayak unattended overnight, so unless you can make advance arrangements for kayak storage

2.0
2.1
2.2
2.3
2.4
2.5
2.6
2.7
2.8
2.9
2.10
2.11
2.12

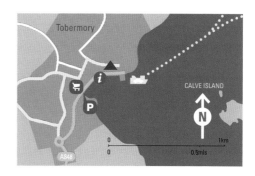

through the Tourist Information Centre or at the Scottish Youth Hostel (01688 302481, www.syha.org.uk), spending the night in Tobermory isn't recommended. Anyway, you have only recently kayaked past some superb wild camping spots, and even more lie ahead.

Should escape be necessary, the small CalMac car ferry to Kilchoan on the Ardnamurchan peninsula departs from the north-east end of the main street. In bad weather, this might be your only escape route. From Kilchoan, there's a once-daily bus service operated by Shiel Buses.

Directions

Follow the north side of Sound of Mull to Dun Ban, then cross to Rubh' an t-Sean Chaisteil on Mull. From there, follow the south side of the sound through a narrow channel between Mull and Calve Island into Tobermory. If possible, land at the beach to right of the harbour wall to eat and re-supply, but due to lack of kayak safe-storage, plan to stay elsewhere overnight.

Sound of Mull – central section

NW stream starts +0500 HW Oban
SE stream starts −0045 1kn springs

Additional information

Tobermory, is the only place on the Scottish Sea Kayak Trail to have a Womble named after it. The name means 'Mary's well' in Gaelic but the place is probably better known to youngsters throughout the UK as 'Balamory'. The brightly painted houses were the backdrop to a BBC television programme

for children, something the locals regard as a mixed blessing. Don't be surprised to spot an under-five year old dragging parents along the main street, looking for PC Plum or Miss Hoolie.

Tobermory town was laid out to the designs of Thomas Telford and built by the British Fisheries Society in 1788, but it never really took off as a fishing port. Tourism came early, and the brightly painted fronts of the buildings, which line its main street, have featured in many a postcard.

A ship from the Spanish Armada is said to have sunk in the bay with a hold full of treasure although, as with such tales, there are several versions. While fleeing from battle in 1588, the *Almirante di Florencia* took on provisions and imprisoned the man who delivered them, Donald Maclean, when he sought payment. As he escaped he started a fire and the ship sank with thirty million ducats on board. Although the vessel now lies below the mud, there have been many attempts to locate the gold. Other tales insist it has already been recovered and reburied in the grounds of Aros Castle.

🕊 Rebellion

To many Highlanders, Scotland was being politically and culturally subsumed by England, first with the Union of the Crowns in 1603 and then the Union of the Parliaments in 1707. The Statutes of Iona in 1609 had required Highland Chiefs to send their heirs to Lowland Scotland to be educated in English-speaking Protestant schools. Some grew resentful that the English Crown was treating their nation as a colony. The Jacobites, as they were known, supported a different royal line, the Catholic Stuarts.

Three times in thirty years, the Jacobites took arms against the English and lost. The most notorious rebellion was led by Prince Charles Edward Stuart, Bonnie Prince Charlie. From France he sailed into the waters of the Scottish Sea Kayak Trail, landing in July 1745. Two months later, Edinburgh surrendered and he held court at Holyrood. A six thousand-strong army marched into England but the English Jacobites did not rise and support them, so in Derby the decision was taken to retreat to Scotland. The Duke of Cumberland pursued them and, on 16th April 1746, totally defeated the highland army on Culloden moor.

Charles fled through the Highlands and, as the song goes, "over the sea to Skye". Despite having a £30,000 bounty on his head, a huge sum, he was not betrayed and was on the run for five months. He was picked up by a French ship (see passage 2.11) and lived the rest of his days in exile.

📷 *Looking to Mull from Camas Nan Geall near Kilchoan.*

2.0
2.1
2.2
2.3
2.4
2.5
2.6
2.7
2.8
2.9
2.10
2.11
2.12

2.6 To Kilchoan (11km*)

When you are tucked safely into Tobermory Bay, it's difficult to see what the weather is like around the corner where you are headed. The local advice is to look north-east, and if waves are breaking on two rocks, Big and Little Stirk, then the sea is rough. After the relative shelter of the Sound of Mull, the trail is now exposed to the full force of the Atlantic, as it heads to Ardnamurchan Point. If the weather is good, then head straight for the point and beyond (see passage 2.7). However, if you have any doubts about this exposed crossing, then head first for the village of Kilchoan. Depending upon the weather, you can either kayak 11km directly across, or add 4km and travel a lovely route via Auliston Point and Maclean's Nose. Either way, it's quite a crossing. Don't land at Mingary Pier where the CalMac ferry docks, but head to the jetty in Kilchoan, pronounced 'Kill-Hoe-an'. This is a quiet, friendly village, and although it receives a lot of summer visitors, you should be content to leave a secured kayak unattended for several days, after checking it isn't in anyone's way.

*15km via Auliston Point

Facilities

The Ferry Stores is a small-sized shop (☎ 01972 510201), no longer near the ferry, but has toilets and showers alongside. The Kilchoan House Hotel (☎ 01972 510200, www.kilchoanhousehotel.co.uk) allows camping in its grounds, but you will have to carry all your stuff about 1km along the road.

There's another campsite at the western end of the bay, conveniently near the water with a good path leading up from the shore, but you will have to kayak here as it's too far to walk with kit. It's run by Trevor Potts, who is something of a sea kayaking legend, having made the first recorded kayak crossing of the Bering Strait between Alaska and the former Soviet Union in 1989.

The community centre runs a good café with excellent homemade soup and it's near the hotel. There are a numerous B&Bs and a once-daily bus service during the week operated by Shiel Buses.

Directions – direct route

From Tobermory, follow the Mull coast past Rubh nan Gall lighthouse then, with the hills of Ardnamurchan for transits, head directly across to Kilchoan.

North entrance to Sound of Mull

NW stream starts +0400 HW Oban
SE stream starts –0100 2kn springs

Off Ardmore Point

E stream starts –0200 HW Oban
W stream starts +0300 weak

via Auliston Point

Carefully cross busy Tobermory Bay to the north end of Calve Island, then cross Sound of Mull to Eilean Uillne, behind which lies a ruined fort. Follow the Morvern coast north to Auliston Point and cross to a gorgeous beach, Camas nan Geall, passing the small island of Sligbech Mor. From here, round Maclean's Nose and continue west to Kilchoan. The wind direction, rather than the tidal streams, will exert most influence on this route.

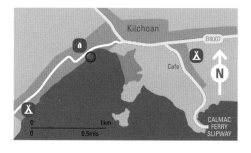

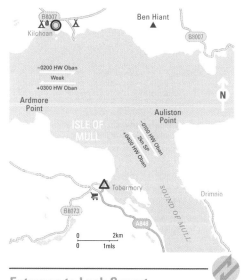

Entrance to Loch Sunart

NW stream starts +0530 HW Oban then turns N
NE stream starts +0030 then turns
E, S and W <1kn springs
This is an approximation as the streams here are rotary, clockwise but weak enough not to make too much difference.

2.0
2.1
2.2
2.3
2.4
2.5
2.6
2.7
2.8
2.9
2.10
2.11
2.12

96

Additional information

A period of Scottish history known as the Clearances took place during the late 1800s (see page 117, 'Knoydart cleared'). Entire families were forced off the land by absentee landowners. The highlanders were crammed onto boats bound for Canada and Australia, their homes burnt or torn down, and sheep were introduced onto the estates. Some Scots helped the landowners carry out the evictions, and apparently, on Ardnamurchan, one such collaborator was Donald MacColl.

According to one book, he threw out of their house a family of six children, their father and his sick, bed-ridden wife. The family survived a few weeks huddled under an old sail until the wife died, cursing McColl, vowing that his soul would be forever in torment and that as proof, no grass would grow on his grave. Donald McColl is reportedly buried in Kilchoan churchyard and it's said that, to this day, you will find only nettles and dock leaves on top of his tomb.

 North to Portuairk & Sanna from Ardnamurchan lighthouse.

2.7 To Sanna Bay (15km*)

In 79AD, a Roman general Agricola was accompanied by the historian Tactius who wrote of Ardnamurchan and Loch Sunart: 'Nowhere has the sea a wider dominion, it has many currents running in every direction; it does not merely ebb and flow within the limits of the shores but penetrates and winds far inland and finds a home among the hills and mountains as though in its own domain.' His description is spot on.

*22km from Tobermory

Height of the otters

The remote 'end-of-the-world' atmosphere of Ardnamurchan is only enhanced by the mystery surrounding its name. According to some books, Ard na Murchan means 'the hill of the great sea' in Gaelic, and that just about sums it up. Ard (in Irish and Gaelic) certainly means a high point, and na means of, but then things get confused. Murchan might be from mùrachan, the plural of mùr (rampart, wall or cliff) or from muirighinn (noise). I sought advice from an expert who told me the most likely derivation is a combination of the words mur or muir meaning sea, and chin or chun meaning dogs, and in this case 'sea-dogs' means otters. So Ard na Murchan, through a convoluted process, is probably Gaelic for 'height of the otters', which is unusual since very few large headlands are named after creatures.

Whatever you call it, to us Ardnamurchan is an isolated finger of rock that you have to get around. It is the most westerly point on the British mainland and the most exposed place on the trail so far. If the sea is calm, and you are starting from Tobermory, head past Rubh nan Gall lighthouse to Ardmore Point on the northern tip of Mull, and then directly across to Sron Bheag on the Ardnamurchan coast. Keep a close look out for dolphins and minke whales. If you are starting from Kilchoan, then Sron Bheag is a short kayak from the jetty.

An exhibition at the lighthouse museum tells the story of 'The Body Snatchers of Sron Bheag'. After a burial at the graveyard, the 19th-century body snatchers would sail into Kilchoan, dig up the body and store it in their cave under the waterfall. Subsequently it would be transported to Edinburgh and sold to the infamous Burke and Hare.

The journey from Sron Bheag to Sanna Bay around Ardnamurchan Point is one of the finest in Scotland. It is deservedly listed in *Scottish Sea Kayaking, Fifty Great Sea Kayak Voyages*, where it is given the most difficult of the three grades. Beyond Sron Beag, huge cliffs leap right out of the sea and there is nowhere to land until after the lighthouse.

> **Tip:** Reception of broadcasts by, and transmissions to HM Coastguard, from handheld marine VHF radios are very limited in this area.

The dramatic coastline seems to become even rougher as you approach the lighthouse, perched high on the headland. Thirty-six metres high and fifty-five metres above sea level, it was designed and built by Alan Stevenson in 1849 of pink coloured granite from Mull. It has a sundial that shows the local time twenty-five minutes after GMT, which proves how far west you are. In any conditions, Ardnamurchan feels like it's on the edge of the universe.

It's a wonderful place from which to gaze back at Mull, look over to the island of Coll or, better still,

set your sights further ahead towards Muck. Soon you will have to decide whether to break free from the Scottish Sea Kayak Trail as described and make the open crossing to Muck and Eigg, or continue following the trail which hugs the mainland.

There are three landing spots on this passage. If you want to visit the lighthouse, then in southerly wind conditions, it's possible to land in the small bay just north of Ardnamurchan Point, unnamed on OS Landranger maps. However, if you need to escape, then it's better to travel 2km further and land at Portuairk, although you would still have a 7km walk back to the nearest bus stop in Kilchoan.

Facilities

The Sonachan Hotel (01972 510211, www.sonachan.com) is less than 3km up the road from Portuairk.

The most spectacular landing spot around here is Sanna Bay. It's not a popular launching site for sea kayakers because it's tricky to get a car close to the water but it's a magnificent place to paddle. Three long, sweeping beaches, divided by skerries, form a series of natural horseshoes, and the dunes are a perfect place from which to watch a Hebridean sunset. Sanna is a magical location, a sweet spot on the earth.

Ardnamurchan lighthouse.

ᐁ When not to kayak

All this sounds lovely, but the harsh reality is you might not be able to kayak around Ardnamurchan Point in strong winds. These are our home waters and we have visited the point on numerous occasions, but when we kayaked the trail, it was too windy to attempt this passage. Instead we followed the shuttle outlined overleaf.

Directions

From Tobermory, head past Rubh nan Gall lighthouse to Ardmore Point, then cross directly to Sron Bheag. From Kilchoan, leave the jetty and head south-west to Sron Bheag. Keep a suitable distance out to sea, away from the coast, to avoid the inevitable clapotis and work your way around to Ardnamurchan Point and beyond. Sanna Bay is a good landing spot but cars cannot drive close to the water. Portuairk is the better landing if you are heading to a vehicle.

Additional information

The site for Ardnamurchan lighthouse was chosen in 1845 and twenty acres of land were bought for just twenty pounds. It took three years to build, with the blocks of granite precision-cut and numbered at North Bay quarry on the Ross of Mull, shipped over, and then slotted exactly into place. It's described as being an 'Egyptian style' lighthouse, which you may not think an appropriate description until you

have seen the Egyptian influences at the tower entrance, the cottage chimneys and the arches near the top of the tower.

During summer months, the last lighthouse keeper is employed by the trust that manages the buildings, to wait at the top of the tower and answer questions from visitors who climb to the curving staircase. The light has been automatic since 1988, switched on and off by a sensor, with its status and that of the other equipment relayed back to the Northern Lighthouse Board's headquarters in Edinburgh. Listening to a first hand account of life at Ardnamurchan lighthouse is fascinating, and well worth the £5 entrance fee, which also includes admission to the exhibition in the buildings where the lighthouse keepers used to live. (01972 510210, www.ardnamurchanlighthouse.com).

On a clear day, the view is simply stunning. The hills of Harris on the Outer Hebrides can clearly be seen, as can Barra Head at the southern end of the chain. The island of Coll seems close enough to swim across, but our interest is taken with the view north along the route of the Scottish Sea Kayak Trail. This is a perfect vantage point to study the immediate choices of landing at Portuairk and Sanna, and then look further ahead to Mallaig.

Ardnamurchan Point is also one of the hot-spots along the west coast for viewing minke whales, dolphins and other marine mammals. The Hebridean Whale and Dolphin Trust (01688 302859, www.hwdt. org), based in Tobermory, record regular sightings off Ardnamurchan, and have nicknamed one Minke whale 'Holey' because his dorsal fin looks like someone has snipped a piece out with a hole punch.

Shuttle information – Ardnamurchan alternative

This long finger of land can present an insurmountable obstacle. The passage should not be attempted in rough conditions and no-one should feel as if they're missing out a vital part of the trail, if unable to kayak around the point. The essence of this trail is the experience of kayaking the west coast, coping with the challenges that arise, and travelling within the limitations of your ability and the weather. There are several options if Ardnamurchan conditions are too rough for you, most of which add to the excitement of your experience.

Sit it out: Spend time in Tobermory or travelling around Mull, or cross to Kilchoan and visit the lighthouse and museum. Unfortunately, strong winds can last more than a week, even in summer, and your precious paddling time will be ticking away.

Call for a ride: Steve MacFarlane, who owns the Glenuig Inn (01687 470219, www.glenuig.com), is a keen sea kayaker and regularly shuttles visiting kayakers around different parts of the area. This service is aimed at guests who stay at his inn, but if you are stuck, Steve will do his best to help.

Shuttle yourselves around Ardnamurchan: Paddle down Loch Sunart to Resipole campsite where you wait while one of your team collects the car from Oban, then together drive ahead and launch at a convenient point a little further up the trail. How far you go depends on how much trail the weather forces you to skip and how fast you need to be able to get back to your car.

Shuttle directions

Kayak east up Loch Sunart to Resipole Campsite, which is excellent for kayakers as it is right on the side of the loch. Catch the early morning bus, operated by Shiel Buses, to the Corran Ferry and make the five-minute crossing to Nether Lochaber, which is free for foot passengers. Walk up to and cross

2.0
2.1
2.2
2.3
2.4
2.5
2.6
2.7
2.8
2.9
2.10
2.11
2.12

100

the main road, and then catch the coach service 918 to Oban where you collect the car. Drive back on the same route, only this time you will have to pay for the ferry crossing. Once you are all together again, continue heading north on the A861. Look for a place where you can safely launch, leave the car and, crucially, return to by public transport. Here are some alternatives:

Loch Moidart: OS 49 GR: 664720. Doirlinn Car Park. This allows you to rejoin the trail as part of Passage 2.10, leaving through either the south or north channel of this beautiful and historic loch. This option is not recommended as the car park now has a 'no overnight parking' sign, although it is frequently ignored. If you do decide to go ahead with this option, twice daily buses from Fort William and Mallaig meet at Lochailort and serve Acharacle. Ask to be dropped off just before the Shiel bridge and you will have a two-mile walk back to the car.

Glenuig: OS 49 GR: 674777. Glenuig Jetty or Inn. This is probably the most convenient launch spot. There's bunkhouse accommodation and food at the Glenuig Inn (01687 470219, www.glenuig.com) which is run by a sea kayaker, a very tiny shop with intermittent opening hours (www.glenuigshop.org. uk), plenty of parking and easy access to the sea.

As before, it's served by twice daily buses from Fort William and Mallaig which meet at Lochailort, then continue to Glenuig. Pick up the trail at 2.11.

Lochailort: Buses serve Lochailort more frequently than either of the other two options. Lochailort Jetty (OS 49 GR: 759813) is tucked in between some bushes and marked by a red lifebuoy in a car parking area beside the road. When you return, you will have to walk to here from the bus stop on the main A830 road, about 1.5km away. Pick up the trail partway through 2.11.

Arisaig: Only skip ahead to Arisaig if you are faced with really rough weather, as you will miss some quality kayaking; and beware, once you are outside Loch nan Ceal the coast is just as exposed as before. However, you could spend a whole day exploring the fabulous maze of skerries and small islands that shelter this loch and make Arisaig a hugely popular kayaking area. Check with the people in the small harbour office if you hope to leave your car in their parking spaces as they often have to move boats around. When you have to return, the bus stops in Arisaig village, while the train station is about 1km above the town. Pick up the trail part way through 2.11 for Arisaig information and 2.12 for the next passage.

 ## Avoiding Ardnamurchan

Faced with several days of high winds, we did not kayak around Ardnamurchan Point. Instead we kayaked up Loch Sunart, landed near the Resipole campsite and asked some friends to drive us to our home near the head of the loch.

The next day we shuttled the car from Oban, then drove on to launch in Loch Moidart. However, our car was not parked overnight because, aided by a brisk tailwind, we made it all the way to Mallaig in time to catch the afternoon bus back again. We then shuttled ahead and left the car in Mallaig.

2.8 To Ardtoe (22km)

It's fortunate that Sanna is such a lovely place because strong winds are common and you should be prepared to sit out several days' bad weather.

In perfect conditions, you might consider leaving the trail and heading out to the islands. You could perhaps kayak round Sanna Point at slack water and catch the flood tide across to Muck and Eigg, before crossing back to the mainland at Arisaig. However, since ideal conditions are rare, and because this is a coastal trail, the suggested route follows the mainland. What's more, the voyage along the north coast of Ardnamurchan is superb.

It is not necessarily the easier option. It might be less of a struggle to batter, head down, into a northerly wind crossing to Muck where you can catch a warm ferry to Mallaig, rather than tackle, in a beam sea, the full force of the northerly crashing into the unprotected north shore of this long, remote headland. Better still, stay in the tent or consider some of the Ardnamurchan alternative options outlined in the previous passage.

Once around Sanna Point, which is often rougher than Ardnamurchan Point, you won't know whether to look at their jagged cliffs on your right, or gaze across to the cluster of islands known as The Small Isles; Muck, Eigg, Rum and Canna.

Fascadale Bay is the first landing place after 8km from Sanna Point, a small rocky beach ringed by a cluster of houses.

A headland the size of Ardnamurchan exerts considerable influence on the sea in every state of the tide, so anticipate rough water all the way to the point of Rubha Aird Druimnich. Tucked in a corner is a superb beach called Camas an Lighe, known locally as the 'singing sands', but unless you have lots of time, cut the corner to Ardtoe. A small network of sandy bays offer shelter whichever way the wind is blowing. In an emergency you could probably hitch a ride from here to Acharacle, from where Shiel Buses run services to Fort William, but there's nowhere in the village to camp and no services.

Directions

From Sanna, round Sanna Point at slack water and allow the ebb tide to carry you down the north coast of this wild, remote peninsula. Savour the views and the exposure but take care, as VHF Radios don't work well around here and there are few people around to see a flare. When you reach calm water, cut across to Ardtoe.

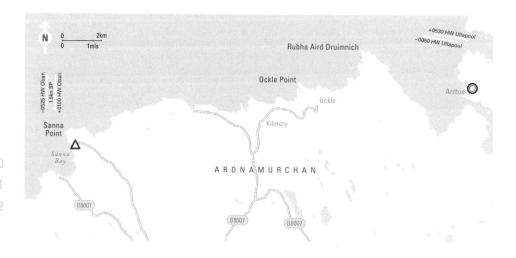

Off Ardnamurchan Point

N stream starts −0525 HW Oban

S stream starts +0100 1.5kn springs

Mid-channel between Eigg and Mainland

NE stream starts +0550 HW Oban

SW stream starts −0010 1kn springs.

Close to Eigg, it's 4kn springs

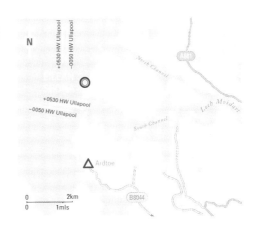

LORDS OF THE ISLES

2.0
2.1
2.2
2.3
2.4
2.5
2.6
2.7
2.8
2.9
2.10
2.11
2.12

2.9 To Eilean Shona (3km)

It's a short, exposed haul up the coast to Eilean Shona where a circumnavigation of this rugged island is recommended. Eilean Shona splits Loch Moidart in two. You enter through the south channel and leave by the north. Exotic trees grown on Eilean Shona were planted by a Captain Swinburn who brought the seeds back from his foreign voyages, only to discover many grew well in the climate of north-west Scotland. The peace and quiet is inspiring, and the island was leased by J.M. Barrie in the 1920s so he could write the screenplay for Peter Pan.

Near the head of the south channel, you come across ruined Castle Tioram (pronounced Cheer-rum), built in the 14th century for Ranald, son of one of the Lords of the Isles, who founded the vast and powerful Clanranald that was based in this castle. Time your diversion to exit Loch Moidart by the north channel at close to high water, otherwise you will get caught in the clawing mud which is exposed at all other times.

Directions

From Ardtoe, follow the coast to a Caribbean-like lagoon at the south-west corner of Eilean Shona which is covered at high water. Only attempt a circumnavigation if you can leave the north channel at close to high water when it's not dry.

Castle Tioram.

Entrance to Loch Moidart South Channel

In stream starts +0530 HW Ullapool

Out stream starts −0050 with fairly strong tidal streams at the entrances

Additional information

Loch Moidart is where Bonnie Prince Charlie reputedly stepped ashore from a French ship in July 1745. Marked on the OS map are seven beech trees, planted to commemorate the seven companions who arrived with the Prince. The giant trees were replaced after the originals were damaged during severe storms in 1988, but it looks like a few are struggling.

Revenge

After the Jacobites were defeated, the English took their revenge. Soldiers sought out Jacobite supporters and laid waste to many a glen in a form of ethnic cleansing. Highlanders were forbidden their dress, music and weapons.

More subtly, they stepped up the process of Anglicising clan chiefs. The chiefs needed money to stand alongside English nobility, so they were given a new way to raise it. The new English laws declared the land belonged to the chief not to his clan, so he could charge rent. In some cases, chiefs raised these rents beyond what was viable. Huge estates were then sold to lowland sheep farmers and English landlords. When they realised sheep were more valuable than people, the hell of the Highland Clearances began.

Throughout the Scottish Sea Kayak Trail, you will find crumbling cottages belonging to what were once small yet successful coastal communities. The main reason you are kayaking past ruins and deserted glens, rather than a thriving, populated coast can be traced directly to the failed Jacobite rebellion.

2.10 To Glenuig (9km)

You are now working your way north, kayaking between small coastal settlements on the way to Mallaig. To the left, there are stunning views out to The Small Isles, particularly Eigg, where the Sgurr rises abruptly from the island. To the right is a rugged coastline with only a few places to land, although one of those places just happens to be a fabulous beach.

Shortly after Loch Moidart's north channel, you reach the skerries of Eilean Coille. These shelter a staggeringly beautiful double beach, cut into a small spit of land, with one beach looking north, the other south, and a saddle of lush grass between. It's a marvellous place to relax, but not to camp as it is also well known to outdoor centres that occasionally bring kayaking groups here.

If you are feeling strong, paddle directly across the Sound of Arisaig to the headland which guards access to the Arisaig skerries, although if you cut this big corner you will miss a couple of places of interest. The village of Smirisary, a short distance ahead, was abandoned during the Clearances, but now some of the houses have been rebuilt and are used as holiday homes. Around the corner, Samalaman Island is graced by yet another beautiful beach, and after that Glenuig Bay. This used to be one of the most remote places in the highlands, reached only by rough tracks or by sea.

Facilities

The Glenuig Inn (01687 470219, glenuig. com) serves food from 8:30am–8:30pm and has a bunkhouse alongside, conveniently close to the water. Provided the kayaks can be secured somewhere off the main road, you may be content to leave them unattended overnight.

There is a very tiny shop with intermittent opening hours (www.glenuigshop.org.uk)

and a once daily bus service during the week operated by Shiel Buses. From Lochailort there's a railway line running west to Mallaig and East to Fort William and beyond.

Directions

Simply keep the land on your right and sea on your left. After Smirisary, consider heading north-west across the Sound of Arisaig, directly to Eilean a t-Snidhe. Alternatively, head east past Samalaman Island into Glenuig Bay.

Off Eilean Shona

N stream starts +0530 HW Ullapool
S stream starts −0050

Additional information

A famous dance was devised in Glenuig called 'The Eight Men of Moidart'. When they learnt Bonnie Prince Charlie, travelling from France and planning to land in their village, the men of Glenuig invented the dance in celebrations. There were only four men and eight were needed, so they jammed their spades upright into the ground to represent their missing partners. After defeat at Culloden, the village was burned and ransacked in 1748 by Red-coats under the command of a Campbell, searching for arms.

2.11 To Arisaig (16km*)

There's a direct route across the Sound of Arisaig to the cluster of islands Eilean a t-Snidhe as before, but this coast is worth exploring close up. In particular, seek out the Iron Age fort which crowns the island of Eilean nan Gobhar at the mouth of Loch Ailort. You can also see 'The Prince's Cairn' in Loch nan Uamh where, after defeat at the Battle of Culloden, Bonnie Prince Charlie fled the highlands for France in September 1746. No roads penetrate the north shore of Loch nan Uamh, and the journey out to the headland is ideal otter-spotting territory. Just before the headland, on a small hill above Eilean a' Ghaill, are the remains of another ancient fort, where you can sit and wonder at the seafaring abilities of the people who called this home, thousands of years ago.

Once around Rubh' Arisaig, you enter the Arisaig skerries. This is some of the most popular sea kayaking in Scotland and on a summer weekend, you will not be alone. Scores of islets offer superb, sheltered paddling in almost all weathers, and maps can't really do justice to the topography that changes minute by minute with the fall and rise of the tide. When the sun shines, white sands turns the shallow water a stunning shade of bright blue and it's easy to convince yourself you are in the Caribbean.

*21km island hopping.

Common seals, or harbour seals as they're also known, love this area and are certain to escort you through the aquatic maze. They give birth in late June and early July, with the young able to swim alongside their mothers within a few hours.

Land in the boatyard in the north-west corner of the bay, using whichever slipway is empty, but before unloading, visit the small office to check you are not in the way. If the yard is busy, there are several places to land along the sea front.

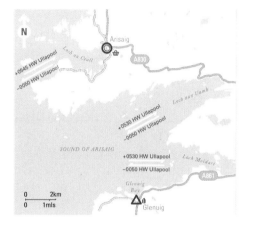

Entrance to Loch Ailort

In stream starts +0530 HW Ullapool

Out stream starts −0050 (fairly strong in narrow entrances to Loch Ailort)

Entrance to Loch nan Uamh

In stream starts +0530 HW Ullapool

Out stream starts −0050 weak

Entrance to Arisaig–Loch nan Ceall

In stream starts +0545 HW Ullapool

Out stream starts −0050

The rule of thirds doesn't apply here. The in stream is strongest during the first half, while the out stream is strongest during the second half, due to the large sandbank between the skerries.

Facilities

In Arisaig, there is a medium-sized Spar store, Post Office, B&Bs, The Arisaig Hotel (01687 450210, www.arisaighotel.co.uk), The Old Library restaurant with rooms (01687 450651, www.oldlibrary.co.uk) and the Café Rhu (01687 450707). Be cautious about leaving an unsecured kayak unattended overnight and seek local advice. The train station is in a ten-minute walk uphill, with direct services to Mallaig and Fort William.

Additional information

The Arisaig skerries also feature in the Pesda Press publication *Scottish Sea Kayaking, Fifty Great Sea Kayak Voyages* where the authors give the route the easiest grade. They describe it as a truly magical place where you can lose yourself for hours, watching the wildlife. If you intend to do this, try landing on one of the beaches on the eastern side of Luinga Mhor or Luinga Bheag and keeping a close eye on your boat as the tide rises. Small ferries, fishing boats and pleasure craft come and go by both south and north channels, so care is needed when travelling to and from the outlying skerries.

📷 *The Arisaig skerries.*

2.12 To Mallaig (15km)

If you leave Arisaig at high water, there's an interesting short-cut between Eilean Ighe and the mainland, through which you will find clusters of mussels clinging to the rocks. Now it's a case of heading north, kayaking from one cluster of skerries to the next, allowing wind and tide to determine whether you pass on the outside or inside. A series of caravan parks line the shore and, on a hot summer day, you will see families playing at the water's edge. The beaches are beautiful, and when a newspaper asked the actor Ewan McGregor his favourite place in the world he reportedly replied, "Camas an Daraich beach near Arisaig".

Facilities

If you are looking for a formal campsite, where you can shower and sort equipment, there are six to choose from; Camusdarach (01687 450221); Gorten Sands (01687 450283); the small Invercaimbe Croft which doesn't take tent bookings but might squeeze you in (01687 450 375, invercaimbecaravansite.co.uk); and three more sites in-between.

Before the days of package holidays, Morar was one of Scotland's top tourist destinations, its principle attraction being the sparkling white sand in the bay. There are still hotels and guest houses in the small settlement, although a new, elevated road has cut between the village and the shore. The large drying bay offers a good stopping place unless there is a strong wind from the south-west, conditions which cause the waves to rear up and dump as they enter the shallows.

There's no easy landing place between Morar and Mallaig, and the shallow, rocky sea-bed can create fairly rough conditions in moderate winds. In an emergency, you might manage a landing in Glasnacardoch Bay, although you would probably have to walk through someone's private garden to reach the road.

Mallaig is unquestionably a working port. It is a busy fishing harbour and a ferry terminal, with one CalMac vessel serving The Small Isles, and another crossing over to Skye. A third, smaller ferry service runs into Knoydart. When entering Mallaig harbour, it's worth adopting the tactics used when leaving Oban: wear bright clothing, keep your eyes open and the VHF handy. Make your way through the moored vessels to a concrete slipway in the south-east corner, which is the best place to land a kayak. Line your kayaks along the wall so ribs and tenders from yachts can use the slipway, and you could safely leave them here for an hour or two, but probably not overnight.

Following the advice of local police officers, leaving a kayak unattended for long in Mallaig is not recommended. Instead, you should wild camp further south and kayak to Mallaig early in the morning. If you are continuing on the trail, then re-supply, shower, do your laundry and move on again, aiming to wild camp in Knoydart. If your vehicle is in Oban and you are heading onto Section 3, then leave your vehicle where it is, because it's as easy to shuttle from Kyle of Lochalsh as from Mallaig. If your journey ends in Mallaig, or you must shuttle your vehicle for other reasons, then try to complete it within the day. Kayaks left on a car overnight will attract less attention than those left on the slipway. Amid all the rush to get things sorted, try to make time for a small celebration. After all, you have completed the second section of the Scottish Sea Kayak Trail.

LORDS OF THE ISLES

2.0
2.1
2.2
2.3
2.4
2.5
2.6
2.7
2.8
2.9
2.10
2.11
2.12

Facilities

The best value breakfasts and hot meals are to be found in the Fishermen's Mission (01687 462086). As a Christian charity, it can't advertise, but residents of the Small Isles seem to treat its café as a waiting room before they catch their ferry home. You can also shower and do laundry.

If you decide to stay overnight in Mallaig, there are numerous hotels and guest houses in the town. With the right approach, some close to the harbour might allow you store kayaks in their yards overnight, but these are also the first to fill. Maximize your accommodation options by arriving in mid-week and booking early. There is an independent visitor information centre (01687 462064) and Sheena's Backpackers' Lodge (01687 462764 www.mallaigbackpackers.co.uk) is close to the harbour, tucked above a busy café with a lovely outdoor terrace. Immediately opposite is a medium supermarket, good enough for partial re-supply, with a small–medium supermarket up a neighbouring street.

2.0
2.1
2.2
2.3
2.4
2.5
2.6
2.7
2.8
2.9
2.10
2.11
2.12

Directions

Leave Arisaig and Loch nan Ceall by either the north channel or the short-cut detailed above. Follow the coast north, the only headland of note being Rubha Da Chuain. Consider stopping on one of the many beautiful beaches around Morar, as there's nowhere to land after this. Mallaig slipway is in the south-east corner of the harbour on a bend in the road.

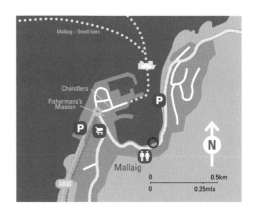

Two miles west of Mallaig

N stream starts +0535 Ullapool

N stream ends with no perceptible S stream –0025

Additional information

Mallaig can be likened to an American wild-west frontier town, a sort of Dodge City with a whiff of fish. In these days of identical high streets, the locals may be proud of this characterisation as it reflects their refusal to conform. It is definitely unique.

Shuttle information

If you have followed my advice, your vehicle is either parked on Oban esplanade or, if you had to use it to shuttle around Ardnamurchan, it is parked at your preferred launch site north of the point.

If you are continuing on the trail and the car is in Oban, the next shuttle will be easier if you just leave it there. If you used it to skip Ardnamurchan, then the decision is not so simple. If the bad weather that forced you to miss out part of the trail is still threatening, then it's perhaps wise to keep the vehicle close to you, so return by bus to the launch spot and bring the vehicle to Mallaig. If you are kayaking under blue skies, leave the car at the launch spot, most of which will be as easy to reach from Fort William in a few days time as from Mallaig.

Learn the etiquette of driving on single-track roads. Passing places are provided every few hundred yards and these should be used to allow oncoming traffic to pass. Indicate and pull in on your side of the road, even if the passing place is on the other side, then wave as the car passes. If you see a vehicle coming up fast behind you, or clearly trying to pass, the same rule applies. Locals get frustrated with visitors who ignore the signs saying 'Use passing places to permit overtaking'.

If you see sheep, slow down. They are kamikaze menaces whose sole aim in life is to leap in front of your vehicle and test the strength of the bumper bar. If you hit one, you are obliged to inform the police.

If you are leaving the trail at Mallaig, the way back to Oban starts with either a bus or train journey to Fort William. The train offers stupendous views along this route, including the Glenfinnan viaduct that features in the Harry Potter films.

Please be aware timetables and services change from year to year, so check transport arrangements. Traveline Scotland has details of almost every bus, rail and ferry service (0871 200 2233 www.

travelinescotland.com) but treat it with caution as it sometimes recommends crazy routes.

Mallaig–Fort William: Take the first train from Mallaig railway station departing 06:06 and arriving in Fort William 07:25 operated by FirstScotrail. If you prefer a bus, it is operated by Shiel Buses (01967 431272 www.shielbuses.co.uk).

Fort William–Oban Bus Station: Turn right as you come out of Fort William railway station, and the small bus station lies along the wall of the large supermarket. Service 918 coach leaves from the far end and the 11:45 direct bus arrives 13:12, operated by Citylink or West Coast Motors. On Saturdays, try to avoid the buses that require you to change in Tyndrum. In Fort William, if you have to wait, the supermarket cafe serves a good value breakfast. If you need equipment there are numerous outdoor stores in the town itself. A kayak store, Nevis Canoes (0845 0945513, www.neviscanoes.co.uk) is a few kilometres out of town on an industrial estate.

Oban Bus Station–Car: In Oban, walk for 20 minutes back along the sea front to your vehicle.

Oban–Mallaig. 2hrs 30min by car: Take the A85 to Connel where you turn a sharp right among houses onto the A828 to Fort William. Later join the A82 at Ballachulish, cross the bridge, and follow the road through Fort William. At the north end of town, at a mini-roundabout, take the A830 Road to the Isles. Some sections of this road are fast dual carriageway, while other sections are slow and single-track. An hour or so later you should be back in Mallaig.

📷 *Approaching Mallaig.*

Duart Castle (page 87).

Loch Sunart (page 96).

Compressor for the foghorn in the Ardnamurchan lighthouse (page 100).

Old Library Restaurant (page 106).

Duart Castle tea shop (page 87).

📷 *Early morning in Sound of Sleat (page 117).*

📷 *Crossing Loch's heaven and hell (page 115).*

📷 *Skye's controversial bridge (page 119).*

📷 *The Jacobite doubles as the Hogwarts Express (page 113).*

📷 *Mallaig harbour (page 113).*

Big Mountains, Big Seas

Section 3: Mallaig – Kyle of Lochalsh (47km)

This is the most spectacular section of the entire Scottish Sea Kayak Trail. Strong kayakers might complete it in a single day, although most will take two or three days to enjoy the magnificent voyage. You may think of this section, not as a journey to undertake on its own, but as an addition to be tagged onto the end of Section 2 or the start of Section 4. Certainly, it is not to be missed.

Here you kayak through big mountain scenery. Across the water, the serrated peaks of the Skye Cuillin rise above the low-lying Sleat peninsula. On the mainland, the gnarly summit of Ladhar Bheinn (pronounced 'Larven') and the other hills of Knoydart dwarf the sea kayaks that pass beneath them. Occasional settlements, all of them remote, huddle at the mountains' feet, and tell a tragic history. This is a landscape that reinforces man's relatively minor place in the natural world, and through which it's a joy and privilege to travel.

OS Sheets:

40 & 33

Tide tables:

Ullapool

Travel to the start

Mallaig is roughly three and three quarter hours drive north of Glasgow, and what a superb drive it is. Follow the A82 alongside Loch Lomond, then climb into the dramatic splendour of the highland mountains. The Black Mount, Rannoch Moor, and the awe inspiring Glen Coe make this a drive to savour. Once through Fort William, turn left onto the Road to the Isles and follow the A830 all the way to Mallaig. This road is gradually being improved but is always a longer drive than expected.

3.0 Mallaig

Mallaig is a busy port all year round and during summer becomes thronged with tourists, most of whom are trying to get somewhere else. CalMac ferries leave to the Small Isles of Muck, Rum, Canna and Eigg, as does the Skye ferry that crosses the Sound

of Sleat to Armadale. Add to these a variety of fishing and fish-farm vessels, other working boats, the Knoydart ferry and pleasure craft, and you're putting to sea in a small, crowded harbour.

There is also a bus and rail terminus where the 'Harry Potter' steam train ('The Jacobite') daily disgorges even more tourists in summer.

Facilities

There are numerous hotels and guest houses in Mallaig, but don't rely on the independent visitor information centre (01687 462064) to find accommodation. Sheena's Backpackers' Lodge (01687 462764 www.mallaigbackpackers.co.uk)

3.0

3.1

3.2

3.3

3.4

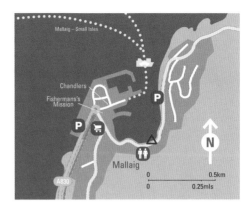

is near the harbour, tucked above a busy café with a lovely outdoor terrace. Immediately opposite is a medium supermarket with a small–medium supermarket up a neighbouring street, but if you're driving here, it's better value to buy supplies in the larger town of Fort William. Johnston Bros chandlery is on the pier (01687 462215). After they park their cars, The Small Isles' residents seem to wait for the return ferry in the café of the Fishermen's Mission (01687 462086), home to 'The best value food in Lochaber', it has been said.

It offers excellent cooked breakfasts until 11.30am, as well as scones, rolls and hot meals until 9pm during the week and until 12pm on Saturdays. They have showers and a laundry service. The outside of the building is rather austere and the inside functional rather than appealing, but the staff in this Christian charity café are friendly and helpful.

Among all the activity, there's only one convenient place to launch a sea kayak and that's from the slipway in the south-east corner of the harbour. If you're starting the trail in Mallaig, then, as you drive into the town, turn right at the mini-roundabout, pass the visitor information centre and, as you pass some public toilets on the left, immediately pull into

one of the short-stay parking bays to unload. The slipway is directly in front. Once the kayaks and kit are safely on the slipway, drive further along the seafront and leave the vehicle in one of the long-stay parking bays, or head back to the mini roundabout, turn left, then right by the police station into another large car-park. Signs in this one proclaim 'No Overnight Parking', but residents of The Small Isles tend to leave their vehicles here for weeks on end. If you want to be certain your vehicle is correctly parked, pass on the details to Mallaig police station (01687 462177).

Two views of Mallaig harbour showing the slipway.

3.0
3.1
3.2
3.3
3.4

Additional information

There was a time in the early 1900s when, it is said, you could walk across Mallaig harbour without getting your feet wet. So many fishing boats were crammed behind the harbour wall, men would reach the shore by stepping from deck to deck. With up to nine men on each vessel, Mallaig was jumping with activity. Previously there had been only a handful of crofts here, huddled at the end of a forty-mile long rough track, until the railway arrived in 1901.

It nearly went somewhere else. Loch Nevis was initially the favoured site for the railway terminal. The west highland line had to reach the sea to bring back the fish caught off the Skye and the Western Isles, and Loch Nevis offered deep, sheltered water. However, a study of the mountain landscape concluded it would be too difficult and costly for a railway line to be cut to Loch Nevis so, despite objections in Parliament that Mallaig would never make a safe harbour, it was chosen as the terminus.

So keen were crofters for the railway to come through, four hundred of them offered to work on its construction and devote a sixth of their wages to buying shares in the scheme. Although growth was limited by its location, squeezed between the railway and the sea, Mallaig boomed.

 ## Cloven hoofed locusts

The failed rebellion of 1745 had far-reaching and long-lasting consequences. Clan chiefs who had risen against the crown forfeited their lands and, in so doing, lost much of their power. Absentee landowners took over, caring little for the people who lived on their estates, focused only on an economic return.

New hardy breeds of sheep appeared around 1760 and, gradually, the best land was given over to these animals. Human communities were pushed onto less fertile land where they clustered around the few spots where food would grow, turning these places into increasingly squalid townships. Some were offered free passage to Australia and Canada. When the 1845 potato famine hit, many were only too keen to sail away. The cruel irony was that people were starving at one end of the Glen, while at the other sheep enjoyed the fertile land. This was the Highland Clearances.

3.1 To Doune – (10km)

Wait until the large fishing vessels have stopped moving in the harbour, and with the VHF handy and tuned to Channel 16, leave quickly through the maze of pleasure craft, keeping close to the east shore. Your view will immediately be drawn to the mountains of the Skye Cuillin, which rise behind the bulk of the low-lying Sleat peninsula (pronounced 'Slate'). Even better views lie around the corner. Keeping close to the coast, turn east into Loch Nevis and gaze up at the imposing mountains of Knoydart. This area suffered badly during the Highland Clearances with thousands of people evicted from their homes.

There is still no road into Knoydart, but the community is recovering well. If you have time, the 12km diversion to visit Britain's most remote pub, The Old Forge at Inverie (01687 462267, www.theoldforge.co.uk) is recommended.

The trail reaches the cliffs of Sron Raineach, swings due north across the wide mouth of Loch Nevis, and makes the crossing, first to Glas Eilean and then to Eilean Dearg. Like Loch Hourn further north, the mouth of Loch Nevis can be fearsomely rough. Sudden squalls blow down from the mountains and whip an otherwise moderate sea into a fury. If you need shelter, it can often be found in Sandaig Bay, not to be confused with the Sandaig Islands further north.

Continue around the steep coastline with no exits until you can escape into the bay at Doune.

No short cut

We tried cutting directly across the mouth of Loch Nevis to Glas Eilean. However, the southwesterly wind whipped up a surprisingly large beam sea, so we went with the waves, travelling a couple of kilometres east of Sron Raineach before heading across to shelter on the other side. We quickly found a campsite and by morning the sea was calm.

Facilities

A remote, rustic hotel is located at Doune and, provided you book in advance for dinner, the owners welcome sea kayakers to camp in the bay. Under Scottish access legislation, you should seek permission if you wish to wild camp within sight of people's houses; so talk to the hotel owners before you set camp in this bay. (01687 462667, www.doune-knoydart.co.uk)

Directions

Leave Mallaig, keeping close to the east shore and curve around into Loch Nevis as far as Sron Raineach. Tidal streams are weak across the wider part of Loch Nevis and Sound of Sleat. Off route, in the narrows heading for Inverie, they reach 0.5kn at springs and there's a good detour into Inverie. If conditions permit, cross directly to Glas Eilean, then to Eilean Dearg. Follow the steep coastline around and escape into the bay at Doune.

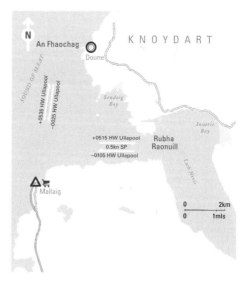

BIG MOUNTAINS, BIG SEAS

3.0
3.1
3.2
3.3
3.4

Loch Nevis

In stream starts +0515 HW Ullapool

Out stream starts −0105 0.5kn springs in narrows

Sound of Sleat

NE stream starts +0535 HW Ullapool

SW stream starts −0025 1kn springs

Additional information

The great mountain landscape of the Knoydart is frequently described as a wilderness yet, less than two hundred years ago, more than a thousand people lived in stone houses along the edge of the sea lochs where they survived by farming and fishing. Knoydart is one of the parts of Scotland where the clearances were ruthlessly effective with almost every family being removed to make way for sheep.

Today, much of the peninsula is owned by the Knoydart Foundation, a partnership of local residents, council and trusts. Although only accessible by boat, the sole village, Inverie, has a growing population of around one hundred people. There is a post office, primary school, B&Bs, bunkhouse and inn.

Until 1853 this was probably a family home.

 ## Knoydart cleared

During the Highland Clearances, the large Knoydart estate was under the management of trustees, its owner having died while his son was too young to assume the responsibility of running the estate. People had been gradually cleared from the estate when, in 1853, the trustees decided to evict them all.

More than three hundred people decided to accept the offer of free passage to Canada on board the *Sillery*, under the condition that their homes were demolished. Those crofters who refused to emigrate were evicted and their houses destroyed. Around thirty people, with nowhere to go, built rough shelters. These were also pulled down, repeatedly, and although some were still squatting on the estate in the summer of 1855, they eventually had to abandon the unequal struggle.

When the Knoydart Estate was sold in 1857 almost all of it was under sheep, frequently referred to as 'cloven-hoofed locusts' or 'the white plague'.

In 1948, an unsuccessful land raid was undertaken by the so-called 'Seven Men of Knoydart'. They attempted to claim ownership of enough land to farm but their case was eventually rejected by the Secretary of State for Scotland. A cairn commemorating the land raid stands in Inverie.

3.2 Sandaig Islands (17km)

Crossing Loch Nevis was a foretaste of what crossing Loch Hourn might be like. Nevis means 'Heaven', Hourn means 'Hell', so if the first was rough, you might want to delay setting out across the second. North from Doune are even more remote houses, some clustered together in the community at Airor, others scattered along the low-lying shore.

When you reach Rubha Ard Slisneach, if the sea ahead is calm and you are enjoying a tail wind and riding the flood tide, then consider striking out on the 6km crossing directly to the Sandaig Islands. Otherwise, enter Loch Hourn as far as the narrows at Rubha an Daraich and cut directly across to Glas Eilean. The tidal streams are weak here but if the wind is blowing against them, they can still become choppy.

Curve around the coast to the beautiful Sandaig Islands which are popular with sea kayakers, other boaters and walkers so are somewhat over-used for camping. Avoid camping here.

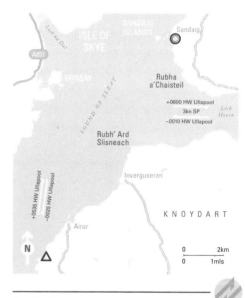

Loch Hourn

In stream starts +0600 HW Ullapool

Out stream starts –0010 HW Ullapool, weak but 3kn spring in narrows.

Sound of Sleat

NE stream starts +0535 HW Ullapool

SW stream starts –0025 HW Ullapool, 1kn springs and 2kn off Sandaig Islands.

Directions

From Doune follow the coast north. If the sea is calm, head directly across to the Sandaig Islands. If slightly choppy, head deeper into Loch Hourn and cross between Rubha an Daraich and Glas Eilean. If very choppy, consider landing and delaying crossing until the tide turns, the weather improves or both.

Additional information

One of the most popular wildlife books of the last century was written on the coast alongside these islands. The Scottish aristocrat, naturalist and shark-hunter Gavin Maxwell lived at Sandaig when in 1960 he wrote *Ring of Bright Water* about how he brought an otter back from Iraq and raised it here. Sandaig was called 'Camusfearna' in the book, which sold over a million copies and was made into a movie starring Virginia McKenna in 1969.

Maxwell's house at Sandaig burned down in 1968 and he moved to Eilean Ban, the island occupied by a lighthouse under the Skye Bridge. Maxwell planned to write a book about British wild mammals and build a zoo on the island, but died from cancer the following year. The Eilean Ban Trust (01599 530040, www.eileanban.org) runs the Bright Water Visitor Centre at Kyleakin. Today there's a white house at Sandaig that is falling into disrepair, and nearby a simple monument marks the site of Camusfearna where Maxwell's ashes are buried.

Why land ownership matters

Leading up to the Highland Clearances, most of the land was owned by absentee landlords who rarely visited and left the running of the estates to their foremen, known as 'factors'. These powerful men gradually took upon themselves most other public offices in their administrative districts and acquired almost untouchable power. One man could be factor, banker and Justice of the Peace, becoming virtually above the law.

Stories are told of cruel factors who would raise a crofter's rent by sixpence on every occasion he didn't touch his cap as a sign of respect to them. Their assistants, so called 'ground-officers', frequently came from crofting families, and were often despised more than the factor himself.

When the landlords decided sheep would be less trouble than people, the factors set about clearing the people with whom they had grown up.

It's easy to see why land ownership remains a powerful issue in Scotland to this day. The Land Reform Bill was one of the first introduced to the Scottish Parliament and, as well as enshrining a right of responsible access (see Overnight), it established rights for communities like Gigha to buy their own land.

Gavin Maxwell's house was near here on Sandaig Islands.

3.3 To Glenelg (8km)

North of the Sandaig Islands, the Sound of Sleat becomes significantly narrower. You can avoid most overfalls by continuing to follow the east shore into the wide curve of Glenelg Bay. The tide has rearranged the shingle to create a mini-lagoon that partially dries in front of Glenelg. The best place to land is near the war memorial, then walk along to the inn to check out your options. There is also informal wild camping in the bay closer to Kyle Rhea, although this is populated by caravans and campervans. If you want to hear live Scottish traditional music, check whether one of the legendary ceilidhs is planned in the village hall and if so, don't miss it.

Directions

From the Sandaig Islands follow the east coast into Glenelg Bay. This is a good place to wait for the tide to set fair in the narrow gap ahead at Kyle Rhea.

Sound of Sleat

NE stream starts +0535 HW Ullapool
SW stream starts –0025 2kn at springs off Sandaig Islands gaining in strength nearer to Kyle Rhea.

Facilities

There's a tiny shop, too small for a full re-supply, several B&Bs and the Glenelg Inn (01599 522273, glenelg-inn.com). It serves meals and the owners might allow you to camp on their land that extends to the beach.

Additional information

Glenelg is the only place-name palindrome on the Scottish Sea Kayak Trail. Its proximity to Skye made it strategically important. For many centuries, cattle drovers swam hundreds of small black highland cattle across here before beginning the long trek to market in the lowlands. The remains of the stone ramp they used can still be seen on the Glenelg side. The beasts which missed the ramp would be washed into Glenelg Bay.

The historian Martin Martin recorded a ferry service here in the late 17th century, and during their tour of the Highlands in 1773, Dr Samuel Johnson and James Boswell crossed to Skye by this route.

Following the early Jacobite risings, the English crown stationed troops in the troublesome highlands. General Wade constructed one of his many military roads, at the end of which was built the Hanoverian barracks of Bernera in 1725. Its remains still stand close to the water. You can't get inside but can approach the ruins on a path alongside a road, confusingly signposted 'No Entry to Bernera Barracks', an injunction intended for motorists.

An hour's walk from the war memorial up Glen Beg are some of the best surviving examples in Scot-

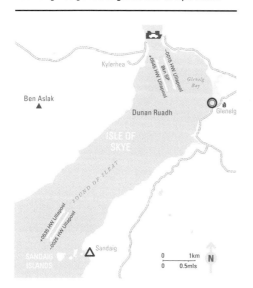

3.0
3.1
3.2
3.3
3.4

land of a type of ancient fortified building known as a broch. Built between 200BC and 100AD during the Iron Age, they were about 10m high and 18m in diameter with double dry-stone walls that left a narrow walkway between, linked by horizontal flat stone lintels. Stairs linked the different levels all the way to the top and, considering they were constructed entirely without mortar, demonstrate a sophisticated level of construction skill.

They appear to be defensive, and could have held off most short-lived attacks, but would have been useless against a sustained siege or large numbers. No one really knows why they were built, what the occupants feared or whether the neighbouring brochs here belonged to friendly or rival groups. There were five hundred of them around Scotland and Dun Telve, the first you come to, is one of the best. Dun Troddan is its neighbour and a few miles' walk further, at the head of the glen, is the galleried Dun Grugaig.

📷 *2,000 year-old Dun Telve.*

Crofting

Crofting is a form of land tenure, agricultural production and, at its heart, a social system that grew out of the clearances.

The people who remained were used by landowners as a casual workforce and were forced to live on poorer land at the coast. Crofting legislation, passed in 1886, gave tenants some security and a reason to improve the land they worked. Although they didn't own it, the area under their control could be transferred within families and to future generations.

The system was based around townships, with individual crofts on the better land and large grazing areas used communally. Crofting is still found in the Western and Northern Isles, and along the west coast mainland in what are collectively called the Crofting Counties. (www.crofting.org)

3.4 To Kyle of Lochalsh (12km)

This is the only passage in Section 3 of the Scottish Sea Kayak Trail where precise tide timing is essential. The tide runs at up to 8 knots through Kyle Rhea (pronounced 'Ray'), a 550m gap between the Isle of Skye and the mainland. Experienced kayakers come here at spring tide when there's an opposing wind to play in the standing waves. Eddy-hopping through here against the early stages of an ebbing neap tide is possible but not recommended at springs with a fully laden touring kayak. When the tide is running in either direction, there are strong eddies on both shores, some running deep into Glenelg Bay. Prolonged winds in the direction of the tidal flow increase the duration of that tidal stream. When winds oppose tidal streams, there are dangerous overfalls to the south and east of the south entrance, but not at the north entrance.

Aim to leave Glenelg just before slack water at the end of the ebb tide and in calm weather. Cross directly to the Skye coast. If the wind is blowing follow the Glenelg coast, but beware of eddies as you near the strait. Time it correctly, and you will catch the north-going stream as it builds. Take great care not to interrupt the work of the small, community-owned ferry which operates here (www.skyeferry.co.uk), and look out for large vessels, using the narrows as a short-cut to save going all the way around the north of Skye.

The light at Sgeir na Caillich marks the end of the tidal excitement, although the stream should carry you west, around the corner, into Loch Alsh. The coast here is the last opportunity to find wild camping until after Kyle of Lochalsh.

Ahead you'll see the great span of the Skye Bridge. Make your way to Rubha Ard Treisnis and Castle Moil, where you have a decision to make. Whether you are leaving the trail or continuing, it is recommended you take a day out here, in either Kyleakin or Kyle of Lochalsh, to shuttle your vehicle. You'll probably spend the night at one of these two places because, whether the car is parked in Oban, Mallaig or one of the launch spots north of Ardnamurchan, the shuttle will take almost a full day. There's no wild camping or formal campsite in the immediate area, but there are other options.

Facilities

Kyleakin has the greatest choice of budget accommodation with three backpackers' hostels. Kayak into the harbour, where the old Skye ferry used to land, and haul your boats out onto the slipway. Although still in use by fishing and pleasure craft, locked, secured boats at the top of the slipway are likely to be safe overnight should you find space in the nearby hostel, Dun Caan Backpackers (01599 534 087, www.skyerover.co.uk) or a neighbouring B&B. The tiny village store is alongside, but Kyle of Lochalsh is a much better place to re-supply and a shuttle bus runs across the bridge every half hour.

There are two other independent hostels next to each other a short walk away: Skye Backpackers (01599 534 510, www.skyebackpackers.com) and Saucy Mary's Lodge above the pub (01599 534 845, www.saucymarys.com). If staying in either of these, consider kayaking around to the shingle beach near the Castle Moil Restaurant and carrying your boats

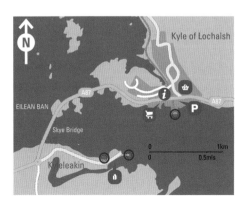

Kyleakin.

3.0
3.1
3.2
3.3
3.4

across to the hostel. These hostels seem popular with busloads of young gap-year backpackers, so they can be lively until the small hours and are a good place for a party. As an alternative, there are lots of B&Bs in the village and an excellent Indian restaurant called Taste of India (01599 534134), which does eat-in and take-away meals, within walking distance along the road to Broadford. If you want to press on to Kyle of Lochalsh, then from Rubha Ard Treisnis, cross to Eileanan Dubha and then pass the commercial piers heading for the old ferry slipway. This whole area is busy with marine traffic so keep a constant look-out in all directions. Head for the large Lochalsh Hotel (01599 534202, www.lochalshhotel.com) and you will find a slipway immediately in front. This is probably the ideal place to stay overnight, as the slipway marks the end of Section 3 of the Scottish Sea Kayak Trail.

'Kyle', as the town is known, has numerous B&Bs, the Kyle Hotel (01599 534204, www.kylehotel.co.uk) and a bunkhouse above Cuchulanns bar (01599 534492), but none are conveniently close to the water. There are no safe spots for leaving unattended kayaks overnight, unless you arrange to have them stored in the grounds of a hotel. Just above the harbour is a Tourist Information Centre and, something you don't see every day, a truly excellent public toilet, an award winner in fact, which has showers, towels and soap.

Directions

Leave Glenelg at slack water, at the end of the south-going stream through Kyle Rhea. If the sea is calm, cross to the Skye coast and follow it until you are picked up by the north-going stream and carried through. In windy conditions, keep to the Glenelg shore but be alert for large eddies as you near the strait. Beware of the small car ferry operating across this gap. Curve around the light at Sgeir na Caillich, by when most of the tidal push will have dissipated. Kayak towards Castle Moil, either to spend the night in a hostel or B&B in Kyleakin on Skye, or cross over to Kyle of Lochalsh on the mainland to organise supplies.

Sound of Sleat

NE stream starts +0535 HW Ullapool
SW stream starts –0025 gaining in strength nearer to Kyle Rhea

3.0
3.1
3.2
3.3
3.4

Kyle Rhea

N stream +05.45 HW Ullapool

S stream –0015 8kn at springs

Strong and prolonged winds from N or S can increase the duration of the tidal stream in the corresponding direction. If the wind is against the tide, expect overfalls at S entrance.

Loch Alsh (east)

In stream starts +0600 HW Ullapool

Out stream starts –0020 Weak

Additional information

Kyle Rhea means 'Strait of the King', while Kyle Akin means 'Haakon's strait', both of which are named after King Haakon of Norway. Defeated at the Battle of Largs in 1263, the Norsemen were limping home when they were ambushed in these narrow passages.

Castle Moil stands on the promontory of Kyleakin and, according to folklore, was built for a Viking princess who married one of the MacDonalds, the Lords of the Isles. Legend has it she was a greedy woman who ordered a huge chain be slung across the Kyle so she could levy a toll from vessels trying to use the short-cut. Her nickname was 'Saucy Mary', a name that has now been appropriated by one of the backpacker youth hostels in Kyleakin.

The story of this underhand, greedy attempt to forcibly extract tolls struck a powerful chord among local people who campaigned against the extortionate tolls charged by the Skye Bridge Company from 1995 until their removal in late 2004. Some people, who were taken to court and convicted for refusing to pay, are still struggling to clear their names.

Kyleakin is a model village, conceived at the start of the 19th century by Lord MacDonald who initially planned a much larger town he would call 'New Liverpool'. The plans were far too grand for the local economy and it was never fully built.

Shuttle information

Whether you are leaving or continuing on the trail, shuttling your vehicle to Kyle of Lochalsh is recommended. It will be parked in Oban, Mallaig, or one of the launch spots north of Ardnamurchan. Please be aware timetables and services change from year to year, so check transport arrangements for yourself. Traveline Scotland has details of almost every bus, rail and ferry service (0871 200 2233, www.travelinescotland.com) but treat it with caution as the website sometimes recommends crazy routes.

Return to Oban

Kyleakin / Kyle of Lochalsh – Fort William: Coach service 915 to Glasgow, operated by Citylink, stops outside the old youth hostel in Kyleakin or the old slipway in Kyle of Lochalsh. Don't even think about using the train, as Kyle is on an entirely different line to Fort William and the journey takes ages.

Fort William – Oban Bus Station: Turn right as you come out of Fort William railway station and the small bus station lies along the wall of the large supermarket. Service 918 coach leaves from the far end and the 11:45 direct bus arrives 13:12, operated by Citylink or West Coast Motors. On Saturdays, try to avoid the buses that require you to change in Tyndrum. In Fort William, if you have to wait, the supermarket cafe serves a good value breakfast. If you need equipment there are numerous outdoor stores in the town itself. A kayak store, Nevis Canoes (0845 0945513, www.neviscanoes.co.uk) is a few kilometres out of town on an industrial estate.

Oban Bus Station – Car: In Oban, walk 20mins back along the seafront to your vehicle.

Oban – Kyle of Lochalsh / Kyleakin: 3hr 15min by car. Take the A85 to Connel where you turn sharp right among houses onto the A828 to Fort William. Later join the A82 at Ballachulish and follow the road north through Fort William to Invergarry. Join the A87 to Kyle of Lochalsh.

3.0
3.1
3.2
3.3
3.4

Learn the etiquette of driving on single-track roads. Passing places are provided every few hundred yards and these should be used to allow oncoming traffic to pass. Indicate and pull in on your side of the road, even if the passing place is on the other side, then wave as the car passes. If you see a vehicle coming up fast behind you, or clearly trying to pass, the same rule applies. Locals get frustrated with visitors who ignore the signs saying 'Use passing places to permit overtaking'.

If you see sheep, slow down. They are kamikaze menaces whose sole aim in life is to leap in front of your vehicle and test the strength of the bumper bar. If you hit one, you are obliged to inform the police.

Return to Mallaig

There are two ways of doing this. You can either travel on the mainland through Fort William, or down Skye and cross to Mallaig by ferry. It's not easy to say which is quickest, but the ferry is the most interesting.

Mainland route

Kyleakin / Kyle of Lochalsh–Fort William: Coach service 915 to Glasgow, operated by Citylink, stops outside the old youth hostel in Kyleakin or the old slipway in Kyle of Lochalsh.

Fort William–Mallaig: Cross the road into Fort William railway station and catch the train to Mallaig with FirstScotrail. Alternatively, take the service operated by Shiel Buses. Walk back to car.

Mallaig – Kyle of Lochalsh: 3hr 15mins by car. Follow the A830 Road to the Isles back towards Fort William. At the mini-roundabout junction with A82, turn north in the direction of Inverness. At Invergarry, turn left onto the A87 to Kyle of Lochalsh.

Skye route

Kyleakin / Kyle of Lochalsh – Armadale: Take the 50 / 55 service to Broadford post office, change and wait for the 51 / 52 / 52C service to Armadale.

Armadale – Mallaig: The Caledonian MacBrayne ferry is popular with tourists and it's rather nice to look back at the coast you have kayaked past. Foot passengers don't have to book in advance and the fare is reasonable. If you enjoyed the trip, you could consider shuttling the car back on the ferry and driving up through Skye.

Return to launch north of Ardnamurchan

At this stage there are simply too many variables to suggest how to return to your car. Return to Fort William or Mallaig by one of the routes outlined above and then, using a copy of the Shiel Buses timetable (01967 431272 www.shielbuses.co.uk), plot your return to Arisaig, Lochailort or Glenelg. Return to Kyle of Lochalsh or Kyleakin by driving to Fort William.

3.0
3.1
3.2
3.3
3.4

📷 *Sandaig Islands (page 118).*

📷 *Castle Moil across Kyleakin harbour (page 123).*

📷 *Sheena's Backpackers Lodge (page 114).*

📷 *Bernera Barracks (page 120).*

📷 *Gavin Maxwell monument (page 119).*

Among the Arisaig Skerries (page 106). Photo | Douglas Wilcox.

📷 A beach called 'Sand' (page 134).

📷 Fractured rock north of Melvaig (page 138).

📷 Red point (page 134).

📷 Rubha Reidh lighhouse, now a hostel (page 138).

📷 Caves of the Summer Isles (page 137).

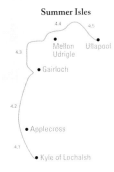

Summer Isles

4.4   4.5

Mellon   Ullapool
Udrigle

4.3

● Gairloch

4.2

● Applecross

4.1

● Kyle of Lochalsh

Northlands

Section 4: Kyle of Lochalsh – Ullapool (156km)

This is the most remote and exposed section of the Scottish Sea Kayak Trail. As you journey north, all shelter disappears and the trail lies at the mercy of wind and swell from almost all points of the compass. It rounds one remote rocky headland after another, each a major challenge that can prove impassable in bad weather. There are only a few villages in which to seek refuge. This is Scotland at its wildest, most wonderful best.

Close to the end comes the significant open water crossing to the Summer Isles, a cluster of around thirty islands. These are the nominal finish of the trail but the practical end, from which you can return to your vehicle, is Ullapool, a day or two paddling further.

Unless you have unlimited time and are prepared to sit out weeks of bad weather, simply starting this section is no guarantee you will complete it. Come to terms with this at the outset and you won't feel a failure if the weather stops you in your tracks.

OS Sheets:

33, 24 19 & 15

Tide tables:

Ullapool

Travel to the start

Kyle of Lochalsh is a four and three quarter hour drive north of Glasgow through magnificent mountain scenery. It covers most of the drive described at the start of Section 3 and adds even more splendour, with panoramic views across Knoydart and the fabulous descent through Glen Shiel. Once you reach Kyle, turn left at the main traffic lights and immediately ahead you will see the old ferry slipway which is where you launch for this section. There are free, long-stay parking bays nearby to the east.

4.0 Kyle of Lochalsh – (0km)

Clustered around the north end of the Skye Bridge, Kyle of Lochalsh is set in a commanding position and was a natural ferry port. Today that original purpose is gone but, with growing numbers of peo- ple moving into nearby communities, 'Kyle', as it's called for short, is reinventing itself as a hub town and tourist destination.

Facilities

You will find a medium supermarket on the main street and a medium–large super- market on the Skye Bridge side of town, enough for a full re-supply. There's a marine store, which is more like a general hardware shop, a selection of reasonable places to eat and a fair range of accom- modation. The Lochalsh Hotel (01599 534202, www.lochalshhotel.com)   and

NORTHLANDS

4.0

4.1
4.2
4.3
4.4
4.5
4.6

the Kyle Hotel (☎ 01599 534204, www. kylehotel.co.uk) are the biggest. Those seeking budget accommodation will find a hostel on the main Station Road, part of Cuchulanns bar and restaurant (☎ 01599 534492). More usefully, there are also hostels across the bridge in Kyleakin, detailed in Section 3, some of which are regularly used by lively parties of gap-year students following the backpacker trail around Scotland. The public toilets next to the Tourist Information Centre have won numerous awards and have showers with soap and towels.

Just to clarify the names of places: Kyle of Lochalsh is on the north side; the stretch of water is called Kyle Akin with the village of Kyleakin on the south side. Around the corner further south is a strait called Kyle Rhea with the village of Kylerhea alongside.

Additional information

There was probably a settlement on the site before 1600 but it was when the road from Inverness arrived in 1819 that Kyle of Lochalsh became the main ferry port for Skye. When the railway arrived in 1897, it also became the main port for Stornoway in the Outer Hebrides. Both roles have gradually been stripped away. Ullapool took over the Stornoway traffic when ro-ro ferries were introduced in 1973, and in 1995 the Skye Bridge opened, allowing tourist traffic to whiz through Kyle of Lochalsh with hardly a glance.

It was a major naval base during World War 2, mainly for minelayers that guarded the western approaches to Britain. Kyle residents were issued with security passes that they would have to produce if stopped in the street to prove they were not spies. Kyle has worked hard to re-invent itself as a place tourists want to explore in its own right, rather than merely a place to catch a boat.

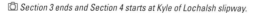
Section 3 ends and Section 4 starts at Kyle of Lochalsh slipway.

4.0
4.1
4.2
4.3
4.4
4.5
4.6

4.1 To Applecross (23km)

This is a fabulous passage. You leave the bustle and noise of Kyle and head to one of the most remote villages in Scotland, perhaps calling in along the way at a group of islands that boast their own natural harbour. All this is done with one of the world's most impressive panoramic views ahead of you, a sweeping vista encompassing Skye, the Cuillin, Raasay and Rona.

Gaelic place-names can be very informative. Kyle of Lochalsh comes from Caol Loch Aillse, which means 'strait of the foaming lake', so you might guess this section of the Scottish Sea Kayak Trail starts in some fast moving water. If you are looking for excitement, and can handle fast moving water, you will love the conditions produced under the Skye Bridge by winds blowing against a spring tide. Fortunately, it's easy to find a sheltered way out of Kyle by cutting inside Eilean Ban and under the elevated section of road that leads to the main span of the bridge.

The Black Islands have some lovely sandy bays and are all the property of the National Trust for Scotland, which owns several small parcels of land around the coast to Plockton. In unsettled weather, hug this coast as far as An Dubh-aird to shorten the exposed crossing to Applecross or to find a wild camping spot to wait for the weather to improve. Otherwise, head north-west from Erbusaig Bay and tackle the 7km crossing directly towards the south west corner of the Applecross Peninsula. The building at Uags is an open shelter maintained by the Mountain Bothy Association.

The Mountain Bothy Association is a charity that maintains more than ninety open shelters in wild places around Scotland, Wales and Northern England with the permission of the landowners. The bothy code is simple.

Respect other users: Leave the bothy clean and tidy with dry kindling for the next visitors.

Respect the bothy: Guard against fire risk. Carry out rubbish you cannot burn, don't bury it. Don't leave perishable food that encourages mice and rats.

Respect the surroundings: Human waste must be buried out of sight, well away from the bothy and water sources. Never cut live wood.

Finally: Don't stay more than a few days. The bothy should not be used by groups of six or more, and during the deer-stalking season, access restrictions should be observed.

At Sgeir Shalach the majesty of the view is almost overwhelming. In good weather, you won't kayak this section fast: you will want to savour the scenery of Skye and its numerous outlying islands. If you have time to detour, many of the best routes around these islands are described in *Scottish Sea Kayaking, Fifty Great Sea Kayak Voyages* by Doug Cooper and George Reid.

A highly recommended short detour is to cross to the Crowlin Islands. Once again, the Gaelic name is descriptive, Cro Linne translating as 'eye-of-a-needle' channel. These three lumps of eroded Torridonian sandstone are divided by a slim channel, through which passage is only possible at high water. That occurs twenty minutes before high water at Ullapool so try to time your arrival. Archaeological excavation has revealed traces of human habitation here an astonishing eight thousand years ago, proving our ancestors knew a good spot when they saw one. Common seals and a few sheep are the only inhabitants now but to explore the remains of the last human settlement, kayak to the sheltered

NORTHLANDS

4.0

4.1

4.2

4.3

4.4

4.5

4.6

east side and land at Camas na h-Annait.

Back on the main trail, from Sgeir Shalach follow the coast north into Applecross Bay. The sand here is the striking red colour of the local Torridonian sandstone and if you attempt to arrive or leave at low water you will see far too much of it: almost the entire bay dries out which can leave you with an exceptionally long carry.

Facilities

If you land to stay at the formal campsite, which has its own small café (01520 744268), then you will have to tackle another carry because it's several hundred yards uphill above the bay. So why land? The answer is food. The family-owned multi-award winning Applecross Inn (01520 744262) is a 'destination restaurant'. People travel for hundreds of miles to enjoy the superb, if slightly pricey, seafood. The outside tables have a stunning mountain and seascape, especially at sunset, and are a wonderful place to relax (when there are no midges). There is also a small food store in Applecross. Mountain & Sea Guides offer sea kayak trips out of Applecross (01540 744394). Information on just about every aspect of the place can be found at: www.applecross.uk.com.

Directions

The time you leave Kyle of Lochalsh isn't particularly important unless you plan to detour to the Crowlin Islands, in which case you should leave two hours forty minutes before high water at Ullapool so it will be high water when you arrive. Work your way under the bridge to the Black Islands, then take a direct line to the Applecross peninsula, heading eventually for Rubha na h-Uamha. In bad weather, head further into the loch before crossing.

Since you are heading north, and it's not yet high tide where you are headed, you might be surprised to find a slight tidal stream working against you. This is because much of the flood tide comes around the north end of Skye, so off this part of the Applecross peninsula it floods in a south-easterly direction.

From Rubha na h-Uamha either detour to the Crowlin Islands or head north to Sgeir Shalach before starting the detour. Pass through the narrow channel between Eilean Meadhonach and Eilean Mor, possibly heading to the east coast of Eilean Mor to visit the abandoned settlement at Camas na h-Annait. To return, cross to Sgeir Shalach and follow the coast into Applecross village.

Crossing to Crowlin Islands.

 ## Tents don't float

The first time we kayaked to Applecross, we camped on the opposite side of the bay. Having pitched our tent we crossed back to the inn for a slap-up meal. We hadn't fully appreciated the distance the flood tide travels and, fed and watered, returned to our tent in the dark to find it rather soggy.

4.0
4.1
4.2
4.3
4.4
4.5
4.6

Kyle Akin

East stream starts –0300 HW Ullapool at springs
and +0100 at neaps. Up to 4kn springs
West stream starts +0330 HW Ullapool at springs
and –0600 at neaps. Up to 4kn springs
The flows here have been measured extensively by
the Underwater Test and Evaluation Centre, based
in Kyle of Lochalsh. The chart has a small tidal atlas
if you wish to calculate the tidal flow precisely.

Between Raasay and Applecross – Inner Sound

N stream starts –0055 HW Ullapool
S stream starts +0505 1kn springs
At south end of Inner Sound, the streams begin
around 45 minutes earlier.

Between Crowlin Islands and the mainland – Caolas Mor

NW stream starts –0010 HW Ullapool
SE stream starts +0550 1kn springs

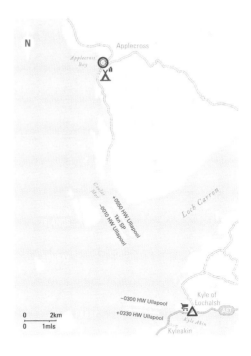

Additional information

The name 'Applecross' is used by locals to describe the whole of the peninsula, while the line
of houses close to the Inn are simply known as
'The Street'. The source of the Applecross name
remains a little confused. It is very different to the
Gaelic place-name 'A' Chomraich', meaning 'The
Sanctuary'. One version is that it's the Anglicisation
of an older Gaelic name 'Abar Crosain' meaning
'mouth of the River Crossan'. Some sources say
that the name was early Latin, or even Pictish. It is
even suggested the place was named after some
apple trees planted in the shape of a cross, but that
seems a little too convenient.

After Iona, Applecross was the second most important Christian site in Scotland. In 673AD, Saint
Maelrubha founded a monastery in what was

then Pictish lands and marked its boundaries with
crosses declaring it a sanctuary. The remains of one
of the crosses is still at Camusterrach farm, and the
parish church, built on the site of the old monastery
in 1817, has a few carved stone fragments. There's
also a Heritage Centre. Saint Maelrubha used his
Applecross monastery as a base from which he
spread the gospel through Skye and the Outer
Hebrides. The sea was the fastest way to travel
in those days, so it didn't matter that, by land, this
peninsula was isolated from the rest of Scotland by
high mountains.

By 1836, the population had grown to around three
thousand. Although many people were shipped
away during the clearances, a lack of work and
opportunity caused others to leave. In the early
1900s, the Applecross Estate was by far the largest
employer but when it cut its number of workers, the
population dwindled still further.

In the 1960s, the local authority suggested evacuat-
ing all the small villages which make up Applecross
and resettling the people elsewhere. This scheme

NORTHLANDS

4.0
4.1
4.2
4.3
4.4
4.5
4.6

sounded too like a second clearance to the high-landers who swiftly, and somewhat indignantly, re-jected the proposal. Instead, a new road around the coast was built, to compliment the high road over the Bealleach na Ba, the 'Pass of the Cattle'. Now most of the three hundred residents of Applecross earn a living from tourism, crofting and fishing.

4.2 To Gairloch 43km

For a place that feels so remote, it is somewhat disconcerting to see the occasional car drive past as you kayak the start of this passage. This is the 'new' road around the coast to Applecross and it soon moves above kayak height and out of earshot. The views across to Raasay and Rona become even more spectacular as the Inner Sound narrows to less than 7km, with the lighthouse at the end illuminating the night sky. If time and weather are in your favour, then a detour around Rona would be a superb trip, as is described in *Scottish Sea Kayaking, 50 Great Sea Kayak Voyages*.

A striking feature of this stretch of coast is the excellent beaches. The first has the inspired name of 'Sand', where archaeologists discovered evidence of a nomadic settlement 8,000 years old. The beaches are a product of the local Torridonian sandstone, a relative newcomer in geological terms, formed under ancient oceans then baked hard in long-gone deserts. The underlying rock is far, far older Lewisian gneiss, some of the oldest rock on the planet. If you see a beach you like, and the surf isn't breaking too hard, pull in for lunch.

However, if the weather is calm, you may be tempt-ed to press on. At Rubha na Fearn, the trail leaves the relative shelter of the Inner Sound and is fully exposed. If conditions are favourable, make the 6km crossing, past Sgeir na Trian, directly to Red Point. If weather or swell make the direct crossing too difficult, then from Rubha na Fearn head south-east into the outer part of Loch Torridon where the crossing is about half the distance.

 ## Inverewe Garden

Not all landowners evicted their tenants during the Highland Clearances. As befit a good highland clan chief, Sir Hector Mackenzie refused to evict a single tenant during this time, despite his estate running at a loss. His sons followed the example when they took over. As a consequence, those evicted from other estates who didn't head to the New World, frequently moved to Gairloch which kept a thriving community while other villages disappeared.

The Mackenzies were also keen gardeners. Osgood Mackenzie created the world-famous In-verewe Garden, four miles outside of Gairloch. This is almost the same latitude as Labrador or St Petersburg, yet the warm Gulf Stream allowed species from around the world to thrive.

Osgood started work in 1870, establishing shelter belts of native and Scandinavian pines and creating a walled garden, using soil from Ireland to reclaim land from the sea. When he died in 1922, he left an internationally acclaimed collection of temperate plants from both hemispheres. The gardens are now owned by the National Trust for Scotland and open all year. Adult entry: £7. (0844 493 2225, www.nts.org.uk). During the summer, there's a regular bus service from outside Strath stores in Gairloch which runs daily, even on Sundays.

4.0
4.1
4.2
4.3
4.4
4.5
4.6

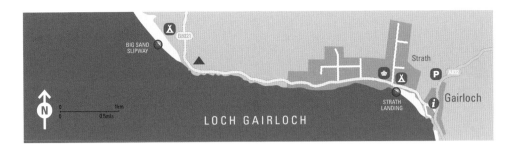

BIG SAND
SLIPWAY

B8021

Strath

STRATH
LANDING

P

A832

Gairloch

N

0   1km
0   0.5mls

LOCH GAIRLOCH

If the sea is too rough even for that, you will have to sit out the storm. With the south side of Loch Torridon occupied by crofts, it might be difficult to find a place to wild camp. So if you can't find a spot, head deeper into sheltered Loch Shieldaig where you will find a semi-formal camping on a grassy area above the village. There's also the Tigh a Eilean Hotel (01520 755251) and several B&Bs.

Red Point is well named. Spectacular, bright red beaches cut into either side of the headland. On the more sheltered south beach, less frequented by visitors, are the remains of an old fishing station, the tall wooden poles on which nets were dried still point towards the sky. There's also a tombolo beach linking the mainland to a lovely flat, grassy island, a perfect place to relax. If you see some flash cars around here, it's because a nearby house was sold to a pop musician who added a recording studio and lives here for part of the year. There's another stupendous beach a little further north at Opinan and beaches all along the front in Gairloch.

All this lovely red sand draws tourists. The collection of settlements, which are known collectively as 'Gairloch', have been a popular holiday destination since Queen Victoria's visit in 1877. Both campsites are busy throughout the summer, though not with royalty these days. Gairloch is the focal point for the outlying community, so although it looks small on the map, there's a lot going on. Which is just as well, because you might have to wait here for good weather to tackle the next passage, one of the most challenging on the entire trail.

Facilities

If you have to spend a day or two in Gairloch the better placed campsite is the Gairloch Holiday Park campsite (01445 712373, gairlochcaravanpark.com), a short walk from the slipway in Strath. The small–medium Strath Stores (01445 72499) is nearby, as is a good café and a couple of restaurants. A thirty minute walk along the sea front takes you past a golf course, several places with internet access, more restaurants, a small museum and 'Britain's smallest commercial local radio station', Two Lochs Radio (106FM & 106.6FM 08707 414657 2lr.co.uk). Eventually you come to Gairloch harbour in the area known as Charlestown.

If you are blessed with good weather and just plan a brief overnight stop at a campsite, then the Big Sand (01445 712152) campsite avoids the detour into Loch Gairloch. Although there's a large, drying beach, there is a convenient slipway near the camping area. There is also a Scottish Youth Hostel at Carn Dearg (01445 712 219 www.syha.org.uk) a few hundred metres away. Yet another slipway can be found on the far side of Caolas Beag beside a house on the water's edge.

NORTHLANDS

4.0
4.1
4.2
4.3
4.4
4.5
4.6

Gales in Gairloch

We landed in Gairloch on a Tuesday afternoon near the end of June, just ahead of a force 8 gale. The wind and rain hammered us for two days, so to pass the time we took a bus and then train to Kyle of Lochalsh and shuttled the car back to Gairloch. A brief weather window was forecast on the Friday but it looked too short to attempt Rubha Reidh. So we launched in Aultbea, hoping to get around Greenstone Point and reach Ullapool in two days. The forecast was wrong. The window slammed shut. We retreated from our attempt, packed our belongings and headed somewhere else for a few days until the weather improved. This can happen anywhere on the trail.

Directions

Cross Applecross Bay and follow the coast north. The beaches are tempting, but make the most of good weather because the exposure to swell and wind increases as you travel north from here. At Rubha na Fearn cross to Sgeir na Trian then the old Fishing Station near Red Point. If this is too exposed, head into outer part of Loch Torridon, where tidal streams are negligible, to either make the shorter crossing or to camp and wait.

After Red Point there are several bright red beaches, all of which are fully exposed to the south, west and north. When you pass Port Henderson,

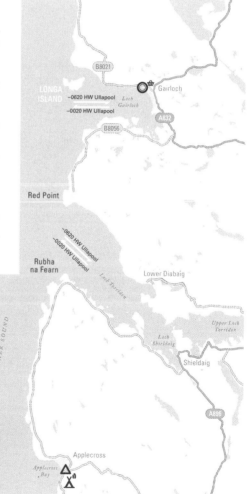

4.0
4.1
4.2
4.3
4.4
4.5
4.6

decide whether you are just going to pass quickly through Gairloch or not. If so, head north directly across Loch Gairloch towards Caolas Beag and a slipway next to the Big Sand campsite (OS: 19 GR: 760778). If you are going into the 'town', aim for the north-east corner of Loch Gairloch and the area known as Strath. Land alongside the slipway in Strath Bay (OS: 19 GR: 796773), close to campsite and supermarket.

Between Raasay and Applecross – Inner Sound

N stream starts –0055 HW Ullapool

S stream starts +0505 1kn springs

Detour – Between Raasay and Rona

NW stream starts –0110 HW Ullapool

SE stream starts +0450 2kn springs

Loch Torridon

In stream starts –0620 HW Ullapool

Out stream starts –0020 weak except in narrows

Loch Gairloch

In stream starts –0620 HW Ullapool

Out stream starts –0020 .5kn springs near land on both sides

Additional information

The archaeological find at Sand provided a wealth of information about the Mesolithic people who lived a nomadic life along this coast. At first the 'midden', or rubbish tip, looked like it was made up of limpet shells, but deeper excavation revealed the remains of other shellfish, fish, animals and birds. Some of the bones had been made into tools and jewellery. The way the debris had accumulated suggested it had piled up very quickly, as if the people had sheltered there one particularly bad winter

and then moved on in the spring. All of which happened a staggering eight thousand years ago. With changes in sea level, the rock overhang is now some distance inland near a car park.

After the Vikings left Gairloch, rival clans, the Macleods and the Mackenzies, fought for two centuries to control the land. In 1494, James IV awarded the area to the Mackenzies and they still own most of the place. Gairloch used to be a major centre for cod fishing, but the harbour is now used for landing prawns, crabs and lobster.

4.3 To Mellon Udrigle (45km)

This is the longest passage on the Scottish Sea Kayak Trail. The intention is not for you to kayak it all in one exhausting day. However, if the weather is good, you must make the most of it and cover longer distances. Big swell or strong winds are not only troublesome around these exposed headlands, they are potentially dangerous.

If the weather is against you, do not attempt this section. In the following section on shuttle information, some alternatives that avoid the worst of the headlands are provided.

The sense of exposure hits the moment you leave Gairloch, and pass inside Longa Island through Caolas Beag. On the horizon you might see the distant Shiant Islands, while looking along the coast you are left in no doubt that the sea is still tearing great lumps out of the sandstone cliffs, geology in brutal action. What were, until recently, small headlands, have had their bases undermined, causing them to collapse forwards, their former flat, grassy plateaus now tilt dramatically towards the ocean. You pass beneath, marvelling at the caves, geos and arches, respectful of the forces that shape them.

Regardless of how this coast appears on the OS map, there are several boulder beaches on which you could land, but the best spot is the long wide sand beach at Seana Chamas where you might just find some flat grass to the south of the impressive waterfall. Further north, where sand returns to boulders, there's a lone house at the water's edge with a slipway alongside. There's a flat grassy spot near here, but it must not be used as a campsite without the permission of the householder. A road leads up to the Melvaig Inn (01445 771212 www.melvaig-inn.co.uk) and this is the starting point for one of the routes in *Scottish Sea Kayaking, Fifty Great Sea Kayak Voyages*.

Your focus must be on getting around Rubha Reidh, a hugely imposing headland that is every bit as serious as Ardnamurchan Point and similarly crowned with a lighthouse. For once, the Gaelic translation

'Smooth Point' is not an accurate description: rounding Rubha Reidh can be anything but smooth. If wind or swell run against the tide, they form heavy and dangerous seas that can extend for many miles off the point. Local advice from the owner of an outdoor centre, based in the hostel at the lighthouse (01445 771263, www.ruareidh.co.uk), is that by keeping close to the coast you avoid the overfalls that lie further out to sea. However, you might come uncomfortably close to some huge, jagged rocks so it's wise to pass here at slack water, ideally as the north-east going stream is about to start, but perhaps even more importantly, pick a day when the wind and swell are at their weakest.

 ## Smooth point

We kayaked to here from Gairloch and aimed to arrive just as the north-east-going stream began. There was little swell and despite a gentle F3 headwind, we arrived at the lighthouse more than an hour ahead of time. Nevertheless, in these benign conditions we easily slipped around the point, even receiving a slight push in places from a stray eddy.

4.0
4.1
4.2
4.3
4.4
4.5
4.6

There is a small bay immediately before the lighthouse and a jetty immediately afterwards, both of which present tricky landings that are almost impossible at low water. The jetty was used to ship supplies to the lighthouse and you can still see the rails along which the provisions were hauled on a truck. Further around the headland is a beach at Camas Mor which, in their book, Doug Cooper and George Reid say "stopping here is a must". You may prefer to spend the time exploring the astonishing coastline between the lighthouse and this beach. Massive cliffs have simply toppled over and crashed into the sea, leaving channels and stacks that only sea kayakers can fully explore. It is an utterly magical place. If you do land at Camas Mor, and if you

are determined to sleep in a bed, then follow the rough track that leads back to the Rua Reidh hostel at the lighthouse base. Otherwise, press on. Follow the coast of this headland, tucking inside Eilean Furadh Mor, through Caolas an Fhuraidh, to eventually reach Sgeir Maol Mhoraidh Shuas.

An unusual hostel beneath Rubha Reidh lighhouse.

Facilities

There are lots of B&Bs in Mellon Charles, Aultbea and Poolewe, and a campsite Poolewe (01445 781 249 www.campingandcaravanningclub.co.uk). Both Aultbea and Poolewe are served by buses.

📷 *Crumbling coast north of Melvaig.*

As you enter the loch, you may notice the old gun emplacement at Rubha nan Sasan, sited here when Loch Ewe was an important naval base. During the Second World War, the merchant ships of the Arctic convoys would load here and wait before making the dash across the Atlantic under naval protection, dodging German U-boats. Even today it is used by NATO, which maintains a large pier near Aultbea.

At this point, if you need to escape, head south into Loch Ewe. If all is well, kayak directly from Sgeir Maol Mhoraidh Shuas to Ploc an t-Slagain and the sandy Slaggan Bay. Once you leave Slaggan Bay there are few places to land until after Greenstone Point. On the map, it looks much like the previous headland, but it is low-lying with none of the high drama of Rubha Reidh. Once around the point, there are several small coves in which you might find wild camping. Otherwise, press on to land on the utterly superb beach at Mellon Udrigle where there's a semi-formal campsite (01445 731343).

The Scottish Sea Kayak Trail began way back near Gigha, rounding remote headlands in exposed seas.

Now the trail is nearing its end amid scenery that could be described with exactly the same words, yet the views and atmosphere are completely different.

Directions

Leave Gairloch through Caolas Beag inside Longa Island and follow coast north. Arrive at Rubha Reidh at slack water, 3hrs and 45 minutes before high water at Ullapool and catch the start of the northeast-going tidal stream. Swell or strong wind from the north may make landing at Camas Mor very difficult, otherwise it's a good spot. Continue along the north coast of the headland to Sgeir Maol Mhoraidh Shuas. In bad weather turn into Loch Ewe to find shelter. Otherwise, cross to Slaggan Bay. Again, try to round Greenstone Point at slack water, about two and a half hours before high water at Ullapool, on the start of the north-going tidal stream, although this is less important than at Rubha Reidh. Catch the eddy back around the headland, then around Rubha Beag to land at Mellon Udrigle and prepare for the crossing to the Summer Isles.

4.0
4.1
4.2
4.3
4.4
4.5
4.6

Loch Gairloch

In stream starts –0620 HW Ullapool

Out stream starts –0020 .5kn springs near land on both sides

Rubha Reidh

NE stream starts –0350 HW Ullapool

SW stream starts +0250 3kn springs

If wind is blowing against the tidal stream off Rubha Reidh, heavy and dangerous seas can form, extending for many miles. Arrive at light at slack as N going stream starts.

Off the entrance to Loch Ewe

NE stream starts –0230 HW Ullapool

SW stream starts +0500 1kn sp

In Loch Ewe

In stream starts –0605 HW Ullapool

Out stream starts –0005 0.5kn springs

Additional information

When the engineer David Stevenson first proposed a lighthouse at Rubha Reidh in 1853, the £5,000 estimate was considered too expensive. By the time the idea was approved in 1908, that estimate had tripled. The tower is 25 metres high and 37 metres above sea level, and the only way to reach it was by sea. People and provisions arrived at the small jetty to the north of the tower, were loaded into a truck, and a steam-powered winch was used to pull it up rails laid on the steep ramp. The truck was then pushed along rails to the tower. The road from Gairloch was not built until 1962 when electricity was installed, along with inside toilets and a hot water system. In 1985, the days of the lighthouse keepers came to an end when the light was made automatic, operated by computer and light sensor, and monitored from Northern Lighthouse Board's headquarters in

Edinburgh. Most of the rails were removed and, as was the practice at the time, just thrown into the sea. They can still be seen, as can a few of the rails still fixed onto the ramp next to the jetty.

The buildings where the lighthouse keepers lived were sold off, and are now an unusual independent hostel (01445 771263, www.ruareidh.co.uk).

Shuttle information – avoiding headlands

Do not underestimate Rubha Reidh. Several teams of skilled and experienced kayakers have had their voyages up this coast disrupted (even abandoned) because of weather conditions on this passage. If the weather is against you, there is no sense of failure in calling a halt to your journey in Gairloch. In many ways it's an alternative ending to the Scottish Sea Kayak Trail.

Before you quit, you might want to try skipping ahead, missing out Rubha Reidh in the hope that Greenstone Point or one of the next headlands will be more manageable. If the weather makes you begin to think this way, it is highly recommend that you try to build time into your schedule to visit the Summer Isles. You might not be able to make the open crossing, but you might be able to drive around through Ullapool, to launch and explore the islands nearest the coast. One day kayaking in the Summer Isles is far better than any number of days sitting in a tent, waiting to get around Rubha Reidh.

Directions

To return to your vehicle in Oban or Mallaig, catch the very early Westerbus service from Strath Stores to Braemore Junction, then board the 961 coach from Ullapool to Inverness. Follow the route described in the grid in 'About the trail' section of this book to reach your car, then drive back to Gairloch.

4.0
4.1
4.2
4.3
4.4
4.5
4.6

140

📷 *Highlands public transport.*

To return to your vehicle in Kyle of Lochalsh, catch the mid-morning Scotbus service 707, usually a minibus, from opposite Strath Stores to Achnasheen. There's an excellent café in Achnasheen where you can wait for the Scotrail train to Kyle of Lochalsh and then walk back to the car. The bus and train journey should take about three hours in total. The fastest return route is to drive via Achnasheen and then Kinlochewe.

Collect boats and equipment and drive further up the trail. Where you launch depends upon the weather and how much of the trail you feel you must skip. Here are some launch options:

To skip Rubha Reidh

If the weather looks too rough, it is possible to launch immediately after the headland in Loch Ewe at two places.

Poolewe: Use the campsite and you can probably launch immediately opposite. This area gets busy with tourists and parking may be tricky. Poolewe is served by a three times a week bus service from Ullapool that necessitates a change at Braemore Junction. The first is with Ewen's Coaches, the second with Westerbus. Check the days and times in advance as they're affected by school holidays.

Aultbea: (OS:19 GR: 865889) A more convenient launch spot is found on the north-west side of Aird Point in Aultbea. Follow signs to Parking and Picnic area, and launch from the wide slipway. The same bus service runs to here as Poolewe and Gairloch.

To skip Greenstone Point

If Greenstone Point seems too much, then move ahead to the next bay. However, the chances are that if you are skipping ahead this far, you won't be able to make the open crossing to the Summer Isles. Are you sure you want to launch here and kayak into Ullapool? Only kayak into Ullapool if you are certain you have enough time to shuttle back and still drive around to launch and explore the Summer Isles.

Laide: (OS: 19 GR: 901921) Here you will find Gruniard Bay Caravan and Camping Park (01445 731225) that is almost on the beach and a good place to launch. If you don't want to use the campsite, take the minor road up the west coast of Gruniard Bay, and immediately stop in the parking area on the right, from where a good track leads to the ruins of the Chapel of Sand and gives beach access.

To skip to the Summer Isles

If at all possible, do not miss the opportunity to kayak among these lovely islands. You might even be able to kayak to Ullapool and catch the bus back. There are three launch spots, each of which require a reasonably long drive through Ullapool to Drumrunie, then along minor roads towards Achiltibuie. If you use any of these launch areas, please park responsibly.

Old Dornie: (OS: 15 GR: 983113) Launch in the shelter of Isle Ristol, then make your way around to the main collection of islands.

Achiltibuie: (OS: 15 GR: 013096) Launch from the beach just east of Achiltibuie pier.

Badenscallie Burial Ground: (OS: 15 GR: 036062) Most useful launch for exploring Horse Island.

4.0
4.1
4.2
4.3
4.4
4.5
4.6

📷 *Summer Isles looking down Loch Broom to Ben More Coigach.*

4.4 To the Summer Isles 20km

The best is saved until last. The Summer Isles are one of the most exciting places to sea kayak in Scotland and there is no better way to arrive than as the climax of your voyage along the Scottish Sea Kayak Trail. Whereas day-trippers can only nibble at the islands, you can cruise between them at your leisure. If you are reading these words just before you launch, you are about to experience one of your most memorable kayaking days ever.

From the long, sandy beach at Mellon Udrigle, head back around Rubha Beag and set a direct course for Priest Island. There is very little tidal stream on this crossing, so your main influences will be the wind and swell which can come from almost any direction. The scenery is stupendous. On a clear day the Outer Hebrides stud the far horizon. Over your shoulder rise the dramatic mountains of the far north, dominated by the bulk of An Teallach. Head for the south end of Priest Island and make your way around the west side, where you will find echoes of the previous day's exploration at Rubha Reidh. The dark red sandstone cliffs have been cut, sliced and diced into caves and all manner of weird shapes. Look for faces in the cliffs and you will find them.

The natural arch at the northern tip is more than just another curve of stone. This is what, as children, we used to call a 'needle's eye', because you can thread your way right through. It is a subterranean kayaking experience, a tunnel through the island's tip. Head south, past more wonderful stone shapes, to the most sheltered landing spot, a boulder beach at Acairseid Eilean a Chleirich.

Priest Island earned its name as a Christian retreat, and a ruined building now stands on the site of an ancient chapel. There are also remains of a prehistoric stone circle, however landing to explore the island isn't recommended. Today a wide variety of seabirds retreat to Priest Island, almost as if they knew it is owned by the Royal Society for the Protection of Birds. Many of these are ground nesting and it would be all too easy to crush eggs or a chick.

Instead, you can play island hop-scotch. From Priest Island you cross to Bottle Island. Cut between Carn Deas and Sgeirean Glasa to Eilean Dubh and then via Sgeir Revan to Tanera Beg. The only problem with Tanera Beg is that both sides are so beautiful, you simply must circumnavigate it. At the south east point you will find a delicate natural arch. At the south west point, there's a massive cave, so big that tourist boats venture inside the mouth. Between Tanera Beg and Eilean Fada Mor, particularly at low water, you will find a lovely lagoon filled with coral sand. With more than thirty islands and islets in the group you really could spend a week exploring.

While no one lives on Tanera Beg, Tanera Mor is inhabited and thriving. Many of the cottages on the island are holiday self-catering lets, there's a sailing centre that runs RYA courses, and a fish farming business operates out of the large bay known as The Anchorage.

Facilities

On Tanera Mor there's a tea shop at the north end of the bay (not the Pier marked on the map), open at around noon during the summer, Monday to Saturday, just before the tourist boats arrive. It doubles as a rather special Post Office, because the Summer Isles has been a fully fledged postal authority since December 1970, and as such is allowed to issue its own stamps. These prove highly popular with collectors (01854 622272 www.summer-isles.com). One particularly attractive set of nine stamps, which are still for sale, issued in June 1996 are based on the Ordnance Survey map of the islands from 1861. They're priced in curious denominations abbreviated to 'SG' and 'PS'. These turn out to be 'Sgillinn', Gaelic for a Scot's shilling, worth one-twelfth of its English pre-decimal counterpart, and 'Punnd Sassanach' or 'English Pound'. Tanera Mor is the only Scottish offshore island to operate a regular, year-round private postal service. Sea conditions permitting, the MV Patricia crosses the sound of Badentarbet three times a week, carrying mail for onward transmission by the mainland post office at Achiltibuie and returns with postal items for island distribution.

Directions

From Mellon Udrigle, return to Rubha Beag then cross 5km to south of Priest Island. Kayak around the west coast, then around the northern tip. Cross to Bottle Island, Eilean Dubh, then to the south end of Tanera Mor. Kayak the west coast, then turn south into the lagoon, the coral sand area between

Tanera Mor and Eilean Fada Mor. The only human habitation is on Tanera Mor at the north end of the large, east coast bay (known as The Anchorage).

To and among the Summer Isles

The tidal streams are negligible in these passages.

In Little Loch Broom (alternative route)

In stream starts –0605 HW Ullapool
Out stream starts –0005 1kn springs in narrows

Additional information

These islands were once used as summer pasture, hence their name. They were a busy place around 1784 when a fishing station was established in The Anchorage on Tanera Mor by the London based British Fishery Society. When the herring fishing was finished, the islanders started illegally distilling whisky. It must have been a pretty lawless place, because in 1900, Tanera Mor was bought by Captain MacDonald, a smuggler who continued his enterprise from these islands. Not surprisingly, there are rumours of buried treasure.

4.0
4.1
4.2
4.3
4.4
4.5
4.6

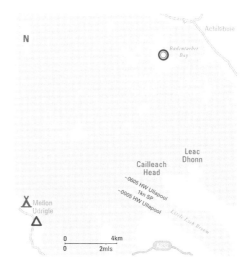

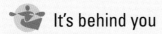

It's behind you

So impressive is the large cave of Sron Ghlas, in the south-west corner of Tanera Beg, you can fail to notice what's going on around you. Perhaps it was the wind drowning out other sounds, or perhaps marine diesel engines are getting quieter, but I was in the mouth of this cave, gazing up at the roof, when I experienced the same sensation you get when someone creeps up close behind and looks over your shoulder. I wheeled around to find the massive bow of a tourist boat almost on top of me, the visitors leaning over the rail and snapping photographs. Not of the cave, but of the startled sea kayaker who had nearly reversed into their boat.

Silver darlings

Since prehistoric times, fishing has been an important source of food for communities along the Scottish Sea Kayak Trail. Between May and September, vast shoals of herring arrived on the west coast and hundreds of boats would take to sea to reap this harvest. In Loch Broom, it's said the shoals of these 'silver darlings' were so dense you could scoop the fish out of the sea by hand.

In the late 1700s, the British Fisheries Society attempted to exploit this on an industrial scale. They built towns virtually from scratch, including Ullapool, and established fish processing stations on the islands of Tanera Beg, Isle Ristol and Isle Martin. Hundreds of ships crowded into the harbours of these islands, ready to export the salted herring around the world. But fishing on this scale was not sustainable. Fifty years after the Society began their plunder, the shoals had thinned and by 1880, the herring had disappeared. The Society went bankrupt and the herring have never returned.

4.0
4.1
4.2
4.3
4.4
4.5
4.6

4.5 To Ullapool (25km)

It might be tempting to rush this last passage. After all, you have explored the Summer Isles and reached the nominal the end of the Scottish Sea Kayak Trail. However, to rush would be a mistake because, anywhere else, the kayak to Ullapool would be a five-star route in its own right.

From Tanera Mor head to Horse Island, which is separated from the mainland by deep water. The trail passes on the mainland side of this island to give easy access to the lovely and popular Scottish Youth Hostel at Achininver, also marked as Achen-

inver on the OS Landranger map.

The view of the mainland is dominated by the impressive Ben More Coigach. It's less than three thousand feet high, but presents an imposing face to the water. There are several small bays along here, but the land is too steep to camp on in comfort. In the distance you will see a couple of white beaches. These are where you are headed. You pass inside Isle Martin, which was given by the RSPB to the community of Lochbroom and Ullapool in 1999. It is a bird sanctuary and if you land, you will find a fairly large settlement of ruined houses among the trees above the main bay. As you near your destination, the beaches you saw in the distance turn out to be, not sand, but composed of small, flat pebbles. Semi-precious stones like amethysts and carnelians can be found near here, provided you know what they look like in their raw state.

After spending so long passing islands, remote headlands and small settlements, the dubious delights of civilisation start to intrude. As you round Rubha Cadail you enter Loch Broom, busy with fishing vessels and the large CalMac ferry which crosses the Minch to Stornoway. Houses dot the coast and there are no more places to camp wild.

You are spoiled for choice when landing in Ullapool. A shingle beach sits in front of the main street, and there's another west of the ferry pier. If you are being collected by a vehicle, then land at the small pier in the yacht club at the east end of the town, or the shingle beach alongside. Although it's a half-mile walk to the bus station, this landing spot is handy for the petrol station and easy to get a vehicle close to load the boats. However, if you have to shuttle back to your vehicle, then landing on the beach which lines the west side of Ullapool Point is better.

Remember to organise a little celebration for yourselves. After all, you have just completed the Scottish Sea Kayak Trail.

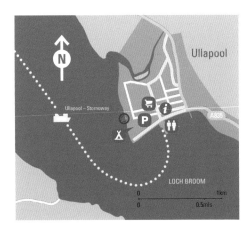

Ullapool harbour.

Facilities

Achininver hostel (01571 844 480, www.syha.org.uk) is just a few minutes' walk inland from the beach and its lovely, remote location makes it very popular in summer months. The twenty beds go quickly, so if you haven't booked, don't expect them to have a spare bed.

If you are looking for a little comfort, continue through Loch Kanaird to a spit of land Aird na h-Eighe, also known as Ardmair Point, where you will find an award winning campsite (01854 612054 www.ardmair.com).

Onward into Loch Broom, land in front of the campsite, Broomfield Holiday Park (01854 612020 www.broomfieldhp.com), a good place to sort your kit, shower and check the bus times. While one of you heads off on the shuttle, the other has somewhere relatively safe to leave the gear while they explore the town. Ullapool is a bustling place, with a large supermarket, bookshop, Tourist Information Centre (01854 612486) and lots of cafes, pubs and restaurants. The sports centre has a swimming pool, showers, a sauna and other aids to recovery. If you are desperate for a bed there are numerous hotels, an independent hostel (01854 613 126 www.scotpackers-hostels.co.uk) and a Scottish Youth Hostel (01854 612254 www.syha.org.uk).

4.0
4.1
4.2
4.3
4.4
4.5
4.6

Directions

Pass north of Horse Island to visit the Scottish Youth Hostel, or to the south for more dramatic scenery. Follow the mainland to north of Isle Martin, then turn south through the narrows in Loch Kanaird. Round Rubha Cadail into Loch Broom, keeping a careful watch for other vessels. Land on the shingle beach in front of campsite and celebrate!

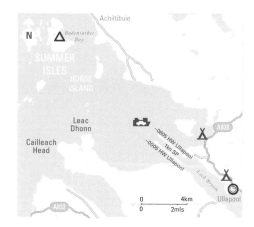

Loch Broom

In stream starts –0605 HW Ullapool
Out stream starts –0005 1kn springs in narrows
Heavy squalls can sweep down the loch during SW winds

Additional information

Unlike most towns, which grow organically, Ullapool was planned and built from scratch, almost like a new town. Thomas Telford created it for the British Fisheries Society in 1788, which explains the grid-like layout and its almost uniform whiteness. When the herring were gone, so was the need for Ullapool and the place took a dive into a collective depression.

In the 1970s, it became home to the Klondykers, the Russian factory ships, around fifty of which would base themselves in Ullapool for six months of the year. Today, there are new fishing boats in the harbour, which is also busy with the twice-daily CalMac ferry service to Stornoway on the Isle of Lewis in the Outer Hebrides. Although the town throngs with tourists in summer, it doesn't have the commercial feel of Oban or Tobermory, but instead, like Mallaig, manages to retain the atmosphere of a working port.

Shuttle information

If you followed my recommendations, your car will either be parked at Kyle of Lochalsh or, if bad weather has forced you to skip some sections, you will have moved it closer. Please be aware timetables and services change from year to year, so check transport arrangements for yourself. Traveline Scotland has details of almost every bus, rail and ferry service (0871 200 2233 www.travelinescotland.com) but treat it with caution as its website sometimes recommends crazy routes.

Tip: Learn the etiquette of driving on single-track roads. Passing places are provided every few hundred yards and these should be used to allow on-coming traffic to pass. Indicate and pull in on your side of the road, even if the passing place is on the other side, then wave as the car passes. If you see a vehicle coming up fast behind you, or clearly trying to pass, the same rule applies. Locals get frustrated with visitors who ignore the signs saying 'Use passing places to permit overtaking'.

If you see sheep, slow down. They are kamikaze menaces whose sole aim in life is to leap in front of your vehicle and test the strength of the bumper bar. If you hit one, you are obliged to inform the police.

4.0
4.1
4.2
4.3
4.4
4.5
4.6

Ullapool – Inverness: Catch the coach service 961 operated by Scottish Citylink.

Inverness – Kyle of Lochalsh: Catch the coach Service 961 operated by Scottish Citylink.

Kyle of Lochalsh – Ullapool: 3hr 30min by car. Take A87 towards Fort William, then turn onto the A890. At the T-junction at the head of Loch Carron turn right, staying on the A890 to Achnasheen, then turn right onto the A832. This is faster than the coast road. At Garve, turn left onto the main A835 to Ullapool. Coming into town, as you pass the filling station, turn left onto the shore street. To return to the campsite, continue past the ferry pier and turn right at the sign to camping, then left into the site itself.

📷 *Nearing trail's end.*

📷 *Formal campsite at Ardmair Point (page 145).*

📷 *Two Lochs Radio, 'Britain's smallest commercial local radio station' (page 135).*

📷 *Below Ben More Coigach (page 144).*

📷 *Catch your own dinner. Photo | Patrick Winterton*

📷 *Find faces in the rock on the way to Ullapool.*

Lunchtime scampi heading into the Applecross Inn (page 132).

📷 *The Lady's Rock, where Elizabeth Campbell was supposedly left to drown P87.*

Afterword

Here, tucked away at the end of this book, I must make a confession which some of you might find startling: this isn't really a trail at all. A 'trail' implies some kind of way-marked or prepared route. In this instance, that is emphatically not the case. Instead, think of this as a virtual trail; a collection of knowledge clustered around a line on a map, to which I invite you to contribute.

Your experience of part or all of the Scottish Sea Kayak Trail may prove valuable to other kayakers. New shops and formal campsites might open, offering additional places to rest and re-supply, while some listed in this book might close. Transport services will change. Sea kayak guides might offer to escort kayakers through sections of the trail, and other related services might develop, such as sea kayak rentals.

So please, share your experience through the website www.scottishseakayaktrail.com. Add to this cluster of knowledge and increase everyone's understanding of how best to enjoy this beautiful coastline in a responsible, environmentally sustainable manner.

Simon Willis
Ardnamurchan, April 2009

Index

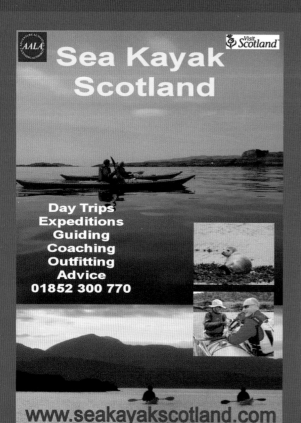